Sociology in Britain

Ernest Krausz

Lecturer in Sociology, The City University, London

Sociology in Britain

A survey of research

With a Foreword by Paul F. Lazarsfeld

Columbia University Press/New York

Published in 1969 by Columbia University Press, New York,
and by B. T. Batsford Limited, London
Copyright © 1969 by Ernest Krausz
Library of Congress Catalog Card Number: 73-90214
Printed in Great Britain by
William Clowes & Sons Ltd, London and Beccles

Contents

v

Acknowledgments

I am very much indebted to the following people who have been most helpful: Professor T. H. Marshall and Dr Michael Young for commenting on the first draft of the book; Professor David Glass and Mr J. A. Banks for commenting on the final draft; my wife Mrs Gillian Krausz and Dr Harold Merskey for editing the book; and Mr Patrick Connell for editorial help and for all arrangements connected with publication. None of those mentioned above are in any way responsible for the shortcomings of this work. I also wish to mention that there were many others who helped readily in sending me reports describing the work of research units. To all of them I am most grateful.

E.K.

Foreword

Many Europeans have written books on American sociology; very few publications tell Americans what sociologists do in other countries. It is therefore highly gratifying that Ernest Krausz has undertaken the arduous task of giving a picture of empirical social research in Britain. There are several reasons why American social scientists should know more about sociology abroad. Most obvious is the importance for the specialist to compare his results with findings in other countries. If they are similar, he can take reassurance from their generality; if studies in two countries—say, on the effect of television—lead to different conclusions, we shall have a rare opportunity to trace the social effects of differing institutions. Comparative research—studies done simultaneously in various countries—serve the purpose of tracing structural effects which are so difficult to investigate. But very often the same goal can be achieved by comparing studies done independently in two or more countries. This book permits the specialist to spot pertinent material in the United Kingdom.

As important as the comparison of results is the comparison of problems. We are all aware how little the sociology of knowledge has been applied to the social sciences. And yet there can be little doubt that the political, economic and moral traditions of a country affect what its sociologists are concerned with. An expert on British and American contemporary history will find in Dr Krausz' review ample material to contribute to an inquiry into the relation between social structures and social science.

Beyond a comparison of findings and problems a third issue should be kept in mind; empirical social research has had a strange history. It is experienced in Europe as an American importation, a good or bad influence, according to the point of view of the beholder. In fact, this is not true at all. The main impetus for sampling came from a desire of British colleagues at the beginning of the twentieth century to repeat the survey of Charles Booth. The use of case studies got its main impetus from the work of the French Le Play at the middle of the nineteenth century. Community studies were a German interest long before any such work was done in the United States.

For two reasons empirical social research is now considered an American specialty. For one reason trends in European sociology were badly retarded by the two world wars which abroad had a much greater impact on the intellectual life than they had in the United States. But a second factor plays an important role. We teach sociology to freshmen and sophomores. This is not done in the European system of secondary education. There are no sociologists in a German Gymnasium or a French Lycée. As a result, the ratio of American to European sociologists is probably about 100 to 1, a ratio reflected in the number of publications, the probability of Europeans needing American scholars and the escalating effect of discussions among United States sociologists themselves. Just for this reason one should be very alert to the following issue: how is the reimportation of American research techniques modified by the intellectual tradition of any specific European country? While Dr Krausz does not raise the question specifically, his story gives leads on how to investigate the matter further.

One of his best leads is his discussion of the various trends among British sociologists. It is not surprising that our colleagues there debate the proper balance between, say, social theory and empirical inquiry. But Dr Krausz shows that the intellectual history of the problem is quite different in the two countries, and thus future conversions may take different forms. In addition the crucial issue of the uses of sociology is bound to take a form different from ours in a country where intermittent labor governments stress the importance of planning.

Anyone who has contact with European scholars is embarrassed when the matter of footnotes is brought up. If we were to count citations in American empirical studies, the references to foreign studies would probably be too small to be noticed by a computer. Dr Krausz' rich material should be followed up as much as possible by American authors. More especially it should be required reading for any American sociologist who goes to an international conference. If we go to a national meeting of the American Sociological Association we know fairly well whom among those who teach at other universities we want to meet. I have pointed out before that we have difficulties when we meet foreign colleagues at international conferences. It takes so much time to find out who is who and what he is working on that we rarely get around to substantive dialogue. We all know a few names of promising sociologists in Britain and elsewhere, but this book affords us a map of British sociologists and universities which should be scanned by anyone who has a chance to meet British colleagues here or abroad.

It is very much my hope that Dr Krausz' example will be followed by other authors. We need similar guides through at least French and German and, I think, Indian sociology. There do exist in various collections brief surveys on sociological trends in other countries. But they cannot possibly go into the details necessary for a real understanding; these Dr Krausz provides so aptly for the British scene. When it comes to Communist countries this lack of information is even worse. Industrial sociology exists on both sides of the Iron Curtain, but the actual wording of questions addressed to workers on comparable topics might be more revealing than the substantive findings of a study on comparable topics.

American sociologists should be grateful to Dr Krausz and the publishers who have provided us with this book.

2 May 1969   *Paul F. Lazarsfeld*

Introduction

With the rapid development of the teaching of sociology in British universities and colleges[1] there has been a concomitant increase in the number of research projects resulting in theses for higher degrees and in the publication of many volumes and articles on different aspects of sociology. The important progress in research that sociology has made was shown clearly by a survey undertaken by the Social Science Research Council in collaboration with the British Sociological Association. According to the Report the number of research projects between 1961–6 more than doubled when compared with the period 1945–60.[2] Little attention has, so far, been paid to the direction that this research is taking and to its contents; this prompted the present writer to examine a substantial proportion of the research work.

As wide a definition as possible will be given here to the

[1] 'Sociology has recently grown with explosive force from two or three centres to practically every university including the new universities and the colleges of advanced technology'—*Report of the Committee on Social Studies* (Heyworth Committee), Department of Education and Science, Cmnd 2660, HMSO, June 1965, para 35, p. 11. In 1967 there were 23,657 applicants for admission to University through the University Central Council for Admissions to read for sociology degrees, as compared with about 20,000 for economics, 21,000 for geography and 9,000 for psychology (combined degrees are not included): see Report of the Hon. Gen. Sec., J. A. Banks, in *Summary of the Proceedings at the Annual General Meeting of the British Sociological Association*, held on 2 April 1968, p. 1.

[2] The number of individuals in research also more than doubled. See *Report on a Survey of Sociological Research in Britain*, submitted by M. P. Carter to Prof. T. H. Marshall, Chairman of the Sociology and Social Administration Committee of the SSRC, July 1967, pp. 7, 8. See also Carter, *Sociological Review*, vol. 16, 1968, p. 18.

term 'research'. It will be taken to mean either any systematic attempt, whether empirical or theoretical, to uncover sociological relationships that have previously been unknown or any critical investigation which adds to our knowledge of society. We will also follow the Heyworth Committee's distinction between 'research' and 'fact-finding' in not accepting routine or administrative fact-finding as true research. It may be noted, however, that as the Committee says this is 'an exceedingly difficult distinction to make, as research may require, or alternatively emerge from, fact-finding exercises or survey'.[1] Another task is that of concentrating on *sociological* research as far as possible, a task made difficult by virtue of the inescapable overlap of sociology with other social sciences.[2] It is recognized in advance that many studies quoted in what follows may not be regarded by the researchers themselves as falling in the narrow academic province of sociology. They were nevertheless selected because undoubtedly they contain sociological material and in some cases because they were essential to a particular argument being pursued.

In view of the above facts and criteria it was decided to review the development in research by considering theses and published volumes and articles that were deemed to have sociological content. It must be stressed that the writing of such a review was envisaged as an introductory exercise. It was necessary, therefore, to limit the review material to a comparatively short period and to the main sources. This also had the advantage of keeping the work to manageable proportions.

The period covered extends from the early 1950s to the late 1960s. This includes, therefore, reports on research more re-

[1] Heyworth Report, *op. cit.*, p. 2.

[2] This is due to the complex nature of human existence. There is an overlap, also, between the social and non-social aspects of life, e.g. between the sociological and medical fields. See Barbara Wootton, *Social Science and Social Pathology*, Allen & Unwin, 1959, p. 17.

cently completed, and it also reflects most of the work done in post-war years. The review thus scans a very important period of development in British sociology. The two main sources used were the *British National Bibliography* annual volumes and the *Index to Theses Accepted for Higher Degrees in the Universities of Great Britain and Ireland*.[1] These sources were not used, however, in their entirety. As far as the first source is concerned only those works were included which met the following requirements. First, that they had a sociological orientation. It was originally felt that only 'core' literature should be included, but some of the titles which are reviewed—although no doubt many sociologists would regard them as part of 'fringe' literature—were accepted on the basis of being sociologically oriented. However, some of the titles found under the classification 'sociology' or under allied disciplines in the *British National Bibliography* were clearly not sociological even in the broadest interpretation. It was simple enough to rectify this by excluding such works. Secondly, only those studies which were carried out by sociologists or social scientists working in Britain and published in Britain were included in the basic material used. Similarly, the vast majority of articles referred to come from British journals, i.e. *British Journal of Sociology*, *Sociological Review*, *Sociology* and *New Society*. The idea was to gain an impression of the sort of encouragement that sociological research was receiving in Britain. Thirdly, where empirical work was involved, only studies on topics concerned with Britain were included. The reason for this was simply the writer's greater familiarity with such studies and topics. It is very much hoped, therefore, that this will not be interpreted as a narrow attitude *per se* towards sociological research.

[1] See *British National Bibliography* volumes, ed. A. J. Wells, published by the Council of the British National Bibliography, British Museum; and *Index to Theses* published by ASLIB.

Turning to the second source the main limitation imposed was the greater difficulty of obtaining theses from provincial universities. Theses presented to the University of London are, therefore, considerably over-represented. Again, the theses included are only for the period 1959–65. The writer tried to ensure, however, that the review of research in most areas was based on a fairly representative and wide range of material. It is true, nevertheless, that there remained the likelihood of some errors of judgment and bias of one sort or another entering into a selection which was subject to the above criteria and limitations. This possibility is admitted and the chapters that follow must be regarded as reflecting the writer's personal views of the trends in sociological research in Britain.

1. The background

No intellectual discipline today is respectable without research. This is so obvious that to labour the point when considering sociology is unnecessary. Before attempting to review some of the sociological research carried out in Britain in the past few years, it is necessary to present a brief discussion of the kinds of framework within which such research can be undertaken and the sort of tools that can be used.

Sociologists disagree about the very nature of their subject, and this naturally is reflected in what different sociologists regard as the most appropriate methods and techniques to be employed in research studies. We shall deal with this debate below. First, however, the distinction which was made between method or framework on the one hand and techniques or tools on the other, must be explained. This distinction is borrowed from T. B. Bottomore who deals with methods 'in the sense of scientific method, or the logic of sociological enquiry' as distinct from research techniques.[1] In fact *methodology* has been defined in the *Dictionary of the Social Sciences* as 'the systematic and logical study of the principles guiding scientific investigation', and it has been pointed out there that it must not be confused with research procedures and techniques.[2]

[1] T. B. Bottomore, *Sociology*, Allen & Unwin, 1962, ch. 3, p. 43, n. 1. In quoting from various writers who do not necessarily distinguish in this way between methods and techniques, the distinction may sometimes be obscured in the discussion that follows; it should not, however, be forgotten. See also this distinction clearly made in W. J. Goode and P. K. Hatt, *Methods of Social Research*, McGraw-Hill, New York, 1952, p. 5.

[2] B. Holzner in Julius Gould and William L. Kolb (eds.), *A Dictionary of the Social Sciences*, Tavistock, 1964, p. 425.

Following Bottomore we can distinguish four principal methods or approaches:[1] the historical, which generally analyses human society and its changes through the broader sweep of historical material; the comparative, which tries to explain social phenomena through a classification of similarities and differences between two or more such phenomena; the functionalist, which stresses in particular the interconnectedness of social institutions, activities and phenomena, and seeks explanations through the analysis of these relationships; and the formal, which is chiefly interested in the forms of interaction in human society rather than in the contents of such interaction. These approaches are, of course, not exclusive, and we often find for instance the historical and the comparative methods used together.

It should be noted that another way of looking at the approach adopted in research is by considering the kind of models used by sociologists. This is not to be confused, however, with the general method used. For it could be argued that in the context of the comparative method, for instance, either the consensus (equilibrium) or the conflict model could be used. Again, the conflict model as well as the integrationist model can be adopted within what is essentially a functionalist approach, by recognizing 'the existence of some overall social system, consisting of those "institutions of the truce" or those organizational means through which conflicts and tensions are managed'.[2]

The techniques fall into three main categories: those which help the preliminary or preparatory stage of the study; those which obtain the basic material for the study; and those which enable the analysis and interpretation of the rough research results. To the first category belong such tools as pre-tests and pilot studies, the examination of other research done in the

[1] *op. cit.*, p. 46ff.

[2] John Rex and Robert Moore, *Race, Community and Conflict*, O.U.P., 1967, pp. 6, 7.

field, experimental designs, and in the case of a sample survey, for example, the preparation of sampling frames, the drawing of the sample, and so on. To the second category belong the techniques of obtaining information through (a) documentary sources, (b) observation, (c) mail questionnaires and other ways of administering questionnaires, (d) interviewing, and (e) contemporary diaries. The tools of the third category range from unstructured examination of the material and simple or cross tabulation, to multivariate analysis, factor analysis, analysis through scalograms, significance tests, etc. The programming and using of computers may also be regarded as techniques which belong to this category.[1]

The debate mentioned above revolves principally around the question of the extent to which techniques borrowed from other sciences should be, or can be, applied to the study of human society. Barbara Wootton, for example, argues that since basically the social sciences do not differ from the physical sciences, such techniques must be applied if any progress is to be achieved. The laws of science, as those of social science, she says, are merely *statements of association* and these are of varying *degrees of probability*.[2] As John Rex puts it, 'It is [now] widely recognized that the arguments of empirical science can never have the same sort of certainty as the rational demonstrations of deductive logic do. Science is not thought of as the search for a set of final and absolute truths. Rather it is seen as an always relatively imperfect and incomplete attempt to explain and to predict the events which we experience.'[3] Similarly John Madge says that 'all knowledge is relative' and the 'search for absolute truth is without

[1] For details of these techniques see, e.g., C. A. Moser, *Survey Methods in Social Investigation*, Heinemann, 1958; and John Madge, *The Tools of Social Science*, Longmans, 1953.

[2] Barbara Wootton, *Testament for Social Science*, Allen & Unwin, 1950, pp. 21ff.

[3] John Rex, *Key Problems of Sociological Theory*, Routledge, 1961, p. 2.

hope'. In any case Madge argues that ultimately empirical truth rests on certain presuppositions or *a priori* truths, so that absolute objectivity cannot be achieved.[1] On the other hand, as Sprott suggests, 'it is not impossible to construct a system of low probability rules of human interaction in terms of which we can make tentative explanations of the past, so far as we know it, and the present, and make modest predictions about the future'.[2]

But if the physical sciences themselves are not on absolutely firm ground in their findings, the social sciences can be even less sure of themselves. Furthermore it appears that sociology is at a greater disadvantage than some other social sciences, such as economics, on account of the greater complexity of its subject matter and generally the danger of subjective involvement of the investigator, the sociologist, in the situation which he investigates.[3] Nonetheless, Barbara Wootton argues for the use of scientific procedures in social investigation even if at the beginning these will lead only to statements of associations with appreciably lower degrees of probability than in the natural sciences. This line is reinforced by views such as those of Bottomore that 'such advances as have been made in sociology have been due to the increasing rise

[1] *op. cit.*, pp. 2–4.

[2] W. J. H. Sprott, *Sociology at the Seven Dials*, Athlone Press, Univ. of London, 1962. On predictions in the social sciences see Michael Young (ed.), *Forecasting and the Social Sciences*, Heinemann for the Social Science Research Council, 1968.

[3] Madge (*op. cit.*, pp. 5, 6) reaches the conclusion that 'social scientists can reduce the extent to which they themselves are infected by the societies that they study, but they cannot eliminate infection'. Similarly, Norbert Elias draws attention to the difficulty of becoming completely detached from the subject one investigates, although it is the task of the professional sociologist to keep apart his role as member of society from his role as investigator of social phenomena. See his article 'Problems of Involvement and Detachment', *British Journal of Sociology*, vol. 7, no. 3, Sept. 1956, esp. p. 238.

of the ordinary methods of science'.[1] In a detailed discussion on 'the logic of social enquiry' Quentin Gibson argues that the features of abstraction, generality, reliance on empirical evidence, ethical neutrality and objectivity—which are the defining characteristics of a science—do apply to the social sciences.[2] What is more important, he shows that there is no real alternative to ordinary scientific procedure which could serve the social sciences.

There are many sociologists, however, who do not put their faith so completely in the application of the methods and techniques of the natural sciences to their subject. They emphasize, for example, the role of insight and understanding in sociology.[3] But T. H. Marshall, who is one of these sociologists, writes that this emphasis 'should not lead to the conclusion that sociology cannot be scientific. It can, but it must be scientific in the manner appropriate to itself, and not by imitation of false models.'[4] Norbert Elias has put forward the proposition that the model generally used in the natural sciences is one where units appear as agglomerations whose interrelationships are fairly simple and loose and whose existence independently of each other would not change their characteristic properties. Against this, the model which appears in sociology is one in which the units form a highly complex system, having a great degree of interdependence to the extent that isolating a unit would result in radical changes taking place in both the unit and the system.[5] He maintains, therefore, that the kind of model used in the natural sciences is not suitable for sociology. In other words these sociologists mainly disagree with the mere imitation of the natural sciences.

[1] *op. cit.*, p. 45.
[2] Quentin Gibson, *The Logic of Social Enquiry*, Routledge, 1960, p. 3.
[3] T. H. Marshall, *Sociology at the Crossroads*, Heinemann, 1963, p. 40.
[4] *ibid.*
[5] Elias, *op. cit.*, p. 243.

More generally, however, they fear, as D. G. MacRae does, that one may fall a victim to 'scientism'.[1] They call for greater sociological imagination,[2] which they say is necessary often for analysing highly intricate and subtle social situations. The most important point of divergence is not so much regarding basic methods. It is generally agreed that these should be scientific.[3] What some say is that certain techniques are applied even when these are not necessary and, worse still, when in fact they are the wrong techniques. Thus MacRae maintains that not everything that is measurable is worth measuring,[4] whilst Elias develops the argument according to which measurement of social phenomena becomes in certain ways almost impossible because of the inextricable interrelationship between the vast numbers of such phenomena which go to make up the whole social system.[5] The use of statistical techniques ought to be limited, therefore, and it has even been suggested that some survey research is expensive nonsense.[6]

Furthermore, S. Andreski, for example, calls surveys and statistical techniques 'prefabricated' and argues that they are both very imperfect and thought-constraining. 'Questionnaires ask only questions adumbrated beforehand by their framers. Forms and tables often induce their users to reject problems which do not fit into them, and in this way function as blinkers. The proneness to these foibles is enhanced by the trend towards research by large teams, where the ubiquitous tendency of a bureaucratic apparatus to stamp out independent thought manifests itself with full force.' Some of Andreski's strictures may be acceptable but it is surprising, to say the

[1] D. G. MacRae, 'Between Science and Arts', *Twentieth Century*, May 1960.
[2] Marshall, *op. cit.*, p. 40.
[3] *ibid.*
[4] D. G. MacRae, *Ideology and Society*, Heinemann, 1961, p. 5.
[5] Elias, *op. cit.*, p. 242.
[6] William Petersen, 'Survey Ambiguities', *New Society*, 24 Feb. 1966.

least, that Andreski regards as unimpressive achievement the
fact that these techniques 'make it easier to avoid certain
errors of observation'.[1] Anything that enables us to avoid
error and bias is a step in the right direction. Similarly it is
curious that Ronald Fletcher in his criticism of 'empiricism'
can go to the extreme of stating that the collection of accurate
facts is not part of sociology.[2] As Tom Burns points out, all
branches of knowledge, and not exclusively the scientific ones,
have as one of their main activities that of fact-finding.[3]
Ernest Gellner has come out in strong terms against those who
disregard empirical evidence and show no concern for the
accuracy of facts, thus basing their interpretations of social
life on philosophical preconceptions.[4] And David Glass has
stated emphatically that the unprofitability of data collection
which is carried out without some guiding purposes, indictable
as it no doubt is, 'does not provide a case for hypotheses
created in vacuo, nor does it sanctify the testing of hypotheses
by using excessively imperfect data and without further scrutiny, or the appeal to support by analogy'. Glass concludes
that 'these are the truisms of research methodology'.[5]

A balanced view is taken by Julius Gould, who on the whole

[1] S. Andreski, *Elements of Comparative Sociology*, Weidenfeld, 1964,
pp. 33–4.
[2] Ronald Fletcher, *Auguste Comte and the Making of Sociology*,
Auguste Comte Memorial Trust Lecture 7, Athlone Press, Univ. of
London, 1966, p. 24.
[3] Tom Burns, *Sociological Explanation*, Inaugural Lecture 28, Univ.
of Edinburgh, 8 Feb. 1966, p. 2.
[4] Ernest Gellner, 'The Entry of the Philosophers', *Times Literary
Supplement*, 4 April 1968, p. 347ff.
[5] D. V. Glass and D. E. C. Eversley (eds.), *Population in History*,
Edward Arnold, 1965, p. 5. We may also note that Bottomore commends
the provision of the exact information for its practical uses and regards this
aspect as a not unimportant contribution of sociological research (see
T. B. Bottomore, 'Sociology' in N. MacKenzie (ed.), *A Guide to the
Social Sciences*, Weidenfeld, 1966, p. 93ff).

argues for greater sociological imagination, but remarks that
'a good deal of effort, very rightly, goes into the study and
refinement of research methods, especially those concerned
with large-scale survey analysis'.[1] But the critics of too
much reliance on statistical techniques argue that, improved
as they must become, these techniques can be regarded as
only some of the many techniques available to the sociologist
who undertakes research. Thus many sociologists advocate
the greater use of participant observation, somewhat on
the lines on which this is used by anthropologists, or the
examination of documentary material and the application to
it of content analysis.[2]

In a different sense John Rex warns against regarding
statistical work as part of sociology proper. Many studies, he
says, which prove statistical correlations between aspects of
human behaviour and a variety of causes are not necessarily
sociological, in that they only pose certain sociological problems which must be further analysed in terms of sociological
theory.[3] But this view can be accepted and yet it need not be
incompatible with the views of E. Grebenik and C. A. Moser.
They say that 'Any attempt to study society must begin with
observation—the collection and gathering of facts and their
interpretation. When these facts concern social groups . . . this
process inevitably entails the use of the statistical method.
Indeed, the beginning of sociology as an empirical discipline is
closely linked with the development of statistics.'[4] These
views are, as we have said, reconcilable. Observation and

[1] Julius Gould, *Penguin Survey of the Social Sciences 1965*, Penguin,
p. 11ff.

[2] See Bryan R. Wilson, 'Analytical Studies of Social Institutions'
in A. T. Welford *et al.* (eds.), *Society: Problems and Methods of Study*,
Routledge, 1962, pp. 104, 108.

[3] Rex, *op. cit.*, p. 190.

[4] E. Grebenik and C. A. Moser, 'Statistical Surveys', in A. T. Welford
et al., *op. cit.*

description must precede analysis—the latter to be made in the light of existing theories and concepts or to elucidate and modify, if necessary, such theories. The more accurate the collection of the facts and their interpretation, the more solid will be the theories which emerge. And there is no doubt that accuracy has been greatly enhanced by the use of statistical tools. At the same time accurate work in itself will not yield sociological explanations—it will simply provide a mass of dry and undigested material. But this may be the lesser of the two evils if compared with highly impressionistic work which relies a good deal on the rule of thumb and the lively imagination of the investigator.

To prevent a reliance on mere impressions, which abound particularly where attempts are made to deal with the subjective aspects of social acts, certain devices have been propagated. Taking the two leading earlier sociologists, we find that Durkheim sought to solve the problem by using objective indices for studying subjective data, whilst Weber advocated the use of 'interpretative understanding'. H. P. Rickman explains succinctly the nature of this specialised technique and argues forcibly that the cognitive process of 'understanding' is unique to the human studies in enabling us to *see through* the meaning or motivation of human behaviour.[1] In fact, the argument goes, the need to understand subjective categories becomes an advantage, for it elicits the use of empathy, and our familiarity with human nature and society allows us to place ourselves, imaginatively so to say, in other social situations and thus to understand them from within. The apparently insoluble difficulty, however, is how to standardize this kind of technique, since without standardization and the possibility of systematic applicability the field thus tackled cannot be checked by other contemporary or future

[1] H. P. Rickman, *Understanding and the Human Studies*, Heinemann, 1967.

researchers and it becomes, therefore, a highly individualistic affair. To argue on the other hand that this is quite compatible with the human studies because of the unique nature of human events, human observations and understanding, would be to succumb to extreme anti-reductionism which would destroy the very *raison d'être* of sociology. Rickman, for one, does not take up this position; the distinctiveness of the human studies, he says, does not controvert the use of the scientific method in the broader sense of that word;[1] the human world, in other words, does lend itself to scientific study.

The three main areas of disagreement, as we have seen, are the questions of how to treat the subjective aspects of social phenomena, whether complete detachment and consequently a 'value-free' approach is possible, and the problem of how to tackle the complex nature of the subject matter. These problems are not unrelated: subjective nuances add, for instance, to the complexity of social phenomena, and detachment is most difficult to achieve where subjective aspects are involved. It is little wonder that reactions to these serious problems have varied and even diverged sharply. Thus at one end, as Elias points out, the view taken may be that 'one has to resign oneself to the use of less precise and less satisfactory methods of investigation in many fields of studies'.[2] At the other end we encounter the retort by Leslie Wilkins that 'It does not follow because a problem cannot be specified by two variables . . . that the problem is insoluble, or that rigorous methods must be replaced by feeling and intuition. . . . The need is to be not more superficial but more systematic in the design of social research.'[3] W. G. Runciman sees part truths in both the positivist and intuitionist claims. Events in the

[1] *ibid.*, p. 62. For a discussion of these problems by non-British scholars see, for instance, H. L. Zetterberg, *On Theory and Verification in Sociology*, Bedminster Press, 1965, ch. 1, 2.

[2] *op. cit.*, p. 242.

[3] Leslie T. Wilkins, *Social Deviance*, Tavistock, 1964, p. 135.

human world are in a sense unique—hence one cannot be a thoroughgoing positivist—yet causal explanations have validity and the search for laws of human behaviour and social phenomena is warranted.[1]

It would seem somewhat futile to protract this debate without first establishing more clearly what in fact has so far been achieved by sociological research and how it has been undertaken. It is also true that, whatever the emphasis among British sociologists regarding methods and techniques, it must be generally accepted that sociological research is indispensable if the subject is to make any progress. Hence in the following chapters consideration will be given to the kind of research that has been going on in Britain in the recent past, the specific hypotheses or theories that were being tested and the more general topics delved into, the types of general approach found in the work of researchers, the techniques used in their studies, the results in the way of theories formulated or general conclusions reached, and the elements of continuity discernible in the research work that has developed.

[1] W. G. Runciman, *Social Science and Political Theory*, C.U.P., 1963, esp. pp. 10, 11.

2. Topics, problems and hypotheses

In bringing together a large number of studies, one is inevitably led towards some attempt at classification, and with any author there is a risk that the presentation will be influenced by a particular view of society. Whilst this is not the place to discuss at length the best taxonomic approach or the most appropriate theoretical framework, it is important to mention some of the possible vantage points. In studies dealing with particular topics we come across such perspectives as the interrelationship between social institutions,[1] the functioning of social control in different areas of society,[2] or the processes of social change.[3] It is also worth noting that the studies under review show much variation, in that whilst some are mainly sociographic and are not guided by any particular perspective, others focus on a topic from two or three angles.

Writers who have provided a general view of sociology as a discipline have used certain frameworks with theoretical under-pinnings. Thus, T. B. Bottomore looks at social institutions as 'elements of social structure'[4] and then considers the processes of social control and social change. Stephen

[1] See, e.g., F. Zweig's research into the mutual impact of family life and industry in *The Worker in an Affluent Society*, Heinemann, 1961; or Joan Brothers' work regarding the effects of an educational system on a particular religion in *Church and School*, Liverpool U.P., 1964.

[2] See, e.g., M. Banton, *The Policeman and the Community*, Tavistock, 1964; or E. Krausz, *Leeds Jewry*, Heffer, Cambridge, 1964.

[3] The theme of social change runs through many studies. It will suffice here to mention the more obvious ones: Ruth Glass *et al.*, *London—Aspects of Change*; P. Willmott, *The Evolution of a Community*, Routledge, 1963; C. H. Vereker and J. B. Mays, *Urban Redevelopment and Social Change*, Liverpool U.P., 1961.

[4] *op. cit.*, p. 129.

Cotgrove uses the idea of a social system composed of inter-related sub-systems and he too examines separately social processes.[1] In Chapter 4 we draw on these perspectives using the underlying framework or pattern of the social structure with its different elements at work, including both institutions and processes. But the 10 sections of that chapter appear under pragmatic headings and reflect research in areas more fully explored.

For the purposes of this chapter, however, a broader discernible pattern may be adequate. Thus, quite a number of studies are known as 'community studies' because, although they often pay special attention to certain aspects of the community or society they investigate, basically the searchlight is focused on the entire community. This distinguishes them from the very large number of studies which deal with special groups or problems, the essential point being the segmental nature of these enquiries and their greater specificity. The third category that stands out comprises theoretical works. These are not concerned with this or that problem or any one society in particular. Their aim is to arrive at general statements about the workings of human society or at rules concerning the study of society. However broad this pattern, it should be conducive to a fairly clear presentation of the different kinds of topic and problem and the main avenues of research which have attracted the attention of sociologists in recent years. Finally it should be noted that the studies to which we refer here are used merely for illustrative purposes. The selection is in no way representative of all sociological literature and there is no attempt to present a full account of topics, hypotheses and problem areas tackled, an exercise which, even if it were possible, would be pointless. In Chapter 4, however, where the research results are dealt with, a coherent although still incomplete picture is provided.

[1] Stephen Cotgrove, *The Science of Society*, Allen & Unwin, 1967, p. 7.

COMMUNITY STUDIES

First let us look at the main areas of interest of the Centre for Urban Studies as shown by two of the studies it sponsored: *London—Aspects of Change* and *British Towns*. The former covered the following aspects of London life: features of metropolitan growth such as transport and social and economic development; the contemporary structure of Greater London; new communities within the metropolis, e.g. Lansbury and Pimlico; and special segments of London which contained minority groups.[1] The latter examined the urban features of all British towns with populations over 50,000 in 1951. The features looked at included: population size and structure, population change, households and housing, economic character, social class, voting, health and education. The main object of the study was 'to provide a description of towns of various kinds—metropolitan centres, suburbs and dormitory towns, seaside resorts, country market towns, and so forth'.[2]

The Institute of Community Studies was responsible for *Family and Class in a London Suburb* by P. Willmott and M. Young, and *The Evolution of a Community* by P. Willmott. In the first study the main interest was in following up a previous piece of research in the East End of London and to compare life there with that found in the suburb chosen for investigation. The authors found Bethnal Green in the East End to be 'a village in the middle of London' where 'most people were connected by kinship ties to a network of other families, and through them to a host of friends and acquaintances'.[3] Life in this corner of London was lived in a closely-knit community

[1] R. Glass *et al.*, *London—Aspects of Change*, Centre for Urban Studies, McGibbon & Kee, 1964.

[2] C. A. Moser and Wolf Scott, *British Towns*, Oliver & Boyd, 1961, preface by R. G. D. Allen, p. vii, and also p. 7.

[3] Willmott and Young, *Family and Class in a London Suburb*, Routledge, 1960, p. vii.

based on familial and local ties. But this was a working-class community near the city centre, and Willmott and Young wanted to compare it with a suburb containing a high proportion of middle-class people. They picked for this purpose Woodford, and the question they posed for themselves was 'whether such a district would have a different kind of family and community life'. More specifically they asked: 'With the greater mobility their jobs demand, would middle-class people be more isolated from their relatives? Would they be more anxious about status, less sociable with their neighbours?' In effect the researchers set up these generalizations, found in sociologically oriented literature about suburbs, as hypotheses to be tested through the study of Woodford.[1] Subsequently, in the latter study mentioned (that by Willmott) an attempt was made to add the time perspective to the comparisons between traditional older communities and the newer housing estates. At Dagenham, therefore, Willmott delved into the question of whether the isolation from kin and aloofness from neighbours was part of a new way of life or whether it merely reflected a transitional stage. Willmott was particularly interested to discover what social patterns evolved on housing estates, once place and people had sufficient time to settle down.[2]

The different life patterns in the older residential city areas and the new housing estates, often built to replace the slums, occupied the attention of such researchers as J. H. Nicholson,[3] Charles Vereker and J. B. Mays.[4] Nicholson considered conditions in communities, some situated in new towns, others in the planned extensions to certain small towns, and yet others in new housing built to replace demolished areas

[1] *ibid.*, p. viii.

[2] P. Willmott, *The Evolution of a Community*, Routledge, 1963, p. ix.

[3] J. H. Nicholson, *New Communities in Britain*, National Council of Social Service, 1961.

[4] C. Vereker and J. B. Mays, *Urban Redevelopment and Social Change*, Liverpool U.P., 1961.

in large cities. The central question Nicholson asked was whether 'the sense of community, of "belonging" [can] be re-created in the new setting'.[1] Vereker and Mays on the other hand were interested in reasons why some residents of 'the blitzed and blighted locality' of Crown Street, Liverpool, were reluctant to move to new areas despite the 'manifest decay and physical inadequacy' of the district.[2] In order to understand the attitudes to mobility they studied 'the social structure and family life of the district seen against its economic background and living conditions'.[3]

Another study which dealt with new estates and an old city area concentrated on the stresses and strains of developing communities. This was carried out by John Spencer and his collaborators in Bristol, who focused attention on the local community and selected three areas for research, 'two of them housing estates on the periphery of the city, and the third an old central area'.[4] Although 'juvenile delinquency was the initial and the starting point of the Project'[5] the aim of the research was soon broadened to include other stresses and strains reflected in truancy, child neglect and adult crime. Two points are worthwhile noting here: (a) that the problems of developing communities were studied alongside an older area; and (b) that the method employed in this study was that of 'action research' upon which we shall elaborate in the following chapter. In another 'neighbourhood' study, also carried out in the Bristol area, the main interest of H. E. Bracey was to examine the way urban families adjusted to new rural–urban fringe neighbourhoods.[6]

[1] *op. cit.*, p. 13.
[2] *op. cit.*, pp. 8, 9.
[3] *ibid.*, see preface by T. S. Simey, p.v.
[4] John Spencer *et al.*, *Stress and Release in an Urban Estate*, Tavistock, 1964, p. 8.
[5] *ibid.*, p. 24ff.
[6] H. E. Bracey, *Neighbours*, Routledge, 1964, p. ix.

In a study of the impact of large-scale industry on a market town Margaret Stacey considered in particular the changes that occurred in the social and cultural life of the town. The changes wrought by the newcomers brought in by industry, on the traditional aspects of this community was Stacey's chief preoccupation, but in this context all the facets of the community were discussed: population, industry, religion, politics, voluntary associations, housing, neighbours, family and kin, social class and so forth.[1] Another study dealing with the effects of population movements on community life was that by W. M. Williams dealing with a West Country village. The aim here was in particular to discover the effects of rural depopulation on family and kinship.[2] On the other hand, James Littlejohn, although still concerned with a rural community, concentrated his attention on social class and class culture in his study of a Cheviot parish.[3]

So far we have considered studies dealing with local communities. The findings of a large number of such local community studies have been brought together by Ronald Frankenberg, who placed the communities on a morphological continuum, from rural to urban, and tried to show in this way the kind of developments that have taken place in the realm of community life in Britain.[4] There are other studies which look at Britain as a whole and consider the cultural, political, religious and other aspects of the larger community, with

[1] Margaret Stacey, *Tradition and Change: A Study of Banbury*, O.U.P., 1960, pp. v, 165.

[2] W. M. Williams, *A West Country Village: Ashworthy*, Routledge, 1963.

[3] James Littlejohn, *Westrigg: The Sociology of a Cheviot Parish*, Routledge, 1963.

[4] Ronald Frankenberg, *Communities in Britain—Social Life in Town and Country*, Penguin, 1966. Josephine Klein has also looked at many studies of family and community and contrasted the trends and patterns of working- and middle-class life: see her *Samples from English Cultures*, vol. 1, Routledge, 1965.

special attention to the changes and developments that have taken place in British life. Such were the aims of writers like Tom Harrison in *Britain Revisited*[1] or Raymond Williams in *The Long Revolution*.[2] Of a similar nature is the study of *Jewish Life in Modern Britain*, edited by Julius Gould and Shaul Esh,[3] in which developments in a larger community, but one which forms only a section of British society, were placed under scrutiny.

SPECIAL GROUPS AND PROBLEMS

Quite a number of studies in this category are concerned with offenders. Thus Alan Little looked into the life of a Borstal to find out whether the attitudes of inmates to the staff and the system improved, deteriorated or remained the same as a result of training.[4] Gordon Westwood's aim was to provide a description of the homosexual in the community.[5] J. W. Anderson undertook a comparative study of recidivists, first offenders and normal boys,[6] and G. E. Levens followed up the occupational and social mobility of 'white-collar criminals' after their discharge from prison. We shall take this last example to show the kind of assumptions that are often made when determining the line of investigation. Levens assumed, for instance, that because the convicted 'white-collar criminal' showed that in his professional, business or other capacity he

[1] Gollancz, 1961.

[2] Chatto, 1961.

[3] Routledge, 1964.

[4] A. N. Little, 'Borstal: A Study of Inmates' Attitudes to the Staff and the System', unpbl. PH.D. thesis, Univ. of London, 1961.

[5] G. Westwood, *A Minority*, Longmans, 1960, pp. 1, 2. See also M. Schofield, *Sociological Aspects of Homosexuality*, Longmans, 1965.

[6] J. W. Anderson, 'A Study of some of the Psychological Factors Associated with Recidivism', unpbl. M.A. thesis, Univ. of London, 1961.

could not be trusted he would encounter difficulties in acquiring positions of responsibility similar to those held before imprisonment. Hence he tried to find out 'the extent to which the sentence results, or does not result, in stigmatic attitudes towards and social rejection of these men' and whether these difficulties led to further offences.[1] These then could be regarded broadly as the hypotheses set up to be tested.

A comprehensive study of the workings of a penal institution was carried out by Terence and Pauline Morris. Their object was to 'look at the prison of Pentonville as an on-going social system, to attempt to identify its formal objectives and the means of their attainment, to sketch the broad outlines of its social structure, and, by providing a descriptive analysis of its culture, to examine certain aspects of the dichotomy of its latent and manifest functions, that is to study the variations between the intended and unintended consequences of day-to-day behaviour within the institution'.[2] In another piece of research Pauline Morris attempted to bring into relief the influences that imprisonment of the husband has on the family and kinship institutions.[3] The specific hypotheses she tested are mentioned below.[4]

A number of researchers have concentrated on the problems of youth in contemporary society. Some have paid special attention to the problems of delinquency. J. B. Mays, for instance, carried out research to find out whether in 'the substandard neighbourhood' misbehaviour of the boy

[1] G. E. Levens, 'A Study of the Occupational and Social Mobility of "White-collar Criminals" after their Discharge from Prison', unpbl. M.SC. thesis, Univ. of London, 1964, pp. 7–9.

[2] Terence and Pauline Morris, *Pentonville: Sociological Study of an English Prison*, Routledge, 1963, p. 4.

[3] Pauline Morris for P.E.P., *Prisoners and their Families*, Allen & Unwin, 1965.

[4] p. 27.

'arises out of deep and perhaps unconscious psychological disturbances resulting from the influences brought to bear on him in early childhood, or whether this can be said to be the result of more conscious processes of learning which continue up to and throughout adolescence'.[1] David Downes' research was directed towards an examination of the very concept of 'delinquent subculture'.[2] Youth culture, youth problems and the relationship of youth to adult society were the general themes dealt with by writers such as Willmott, Mays and Musgrove.[3] A factual enquiry and limited to 'the sexual attitudes and behaviour of young people aged 15 to 19' was carried out by Michael Schofield.[4]

A relatively large number of studies was found to deal with special problems which can come under the general heading of 'social welfare and administration'. The topics range from family welfare services in new towns,[5] health visiting[6] and social casework[7] to industrial injuries schemes[8] or the social consequences of married women on full-time shift

[1] J. B. Mays, *On the Threshold of Delinquency*, Liverpool U.P., 1959, preface by T. S. Simey, p. vii.

[2] David Downes, *The Delinquent Solution*, Routledge, 1966, p. 255.

[3] J. B. Mays, *The Young Pretenders*, Michael Joseph, 1965; F. Musgrove, *Youth and the Social Order*, Routledge, 1964; P. Willmott, *Adolescent Boys in East London*, Routledge, 1966.

[4] M. Schofield, *The Sexual Behaviour of Young People*, Longmans, 1965, p. 3.

[5] Elaine M. Wilson, 'Family Welfare Services in the New Towns of Harlow and Stevenage', unpbl. M.A. thesis, Univ. of London, 1961.

[6] W. C. Dowling, 'The Ladies' Sanitary Association and the Origins of the Health Visiting Service', unpbl. M.A. thesis, Univ. of London, 1963.

[7] N. Timms, 'Techniques and Viewpoints in English Social Casework', unpbl. M.A. thesis, Univ. of London, 1960; and Beatrice E. Pollard, *Social Casework for the State*, Pall Mall, 1962.

[8] Sume Raychaundhuri, 'Industrial Injuries Schemes in India and Britain', unpbl. PH.D. thesis, Univ. of London, 1960.

work.[1] Some of the studies have been concerned with the place and quality of institutional care in society. Thus Peter Townsend surveyed residential institutions and homes for the aged,[2] one of the main objects of his study being an attempt 'to explain how and why older persons have to give up living at home and what effects an institutional environment has upon them.[3] Brian Abel-Smith looked at the changing role of the hospitals, particularly as concerns the needs and objectives of the medical profession,[4] whilst R. W. Revans has considered staff turnover as a measure of morale in hospitals.[5] Ann Cartwright examined hospitalization problems and considered these particularly from the point of view of the patients, whilst Enid Mills considered the special problems connected with mental patients.[6] One may also mention here the attempts to interrelate the disciplines of sociology and medicine. M. W. Susser and W. Watson explain this development in terms of the fact that many diseases are recognized to be not natural calamities but rather the results of man's economic and social environment which are integral parts of his natural environment. These factors help 'to determine the incidence and prognosis of disease'.[7] Titmuss has con-

---

[1] Caroline Rose Hutton, 'Married Women on Full-time Shift Work: Some Domestic and Social Consequences', unpbl. M.A. thesis, Univ. of London, 1962.

[2] Peter Townsend, *The Last Refuge*, Routledge, 1962.

[3] *ibid.*, p. 3.

[4] Brian Abel-Smith, *The Hospitals 1800–1948*, Heinemann, 1964. See also Robert Pinker, *English Hospital Statistics, 1861–1938*, Heinemann, 1966.

[5] R. W. Revans, 'The Morale and Effectiveness of General Hospitals', in G. McLachlan (ed.), *Problems and Progress in Medical Care: Essays on Current Research*, O.U.P., for the Nuffield Provincial Hospitals Trust, 1964.

[6] Ann Cartwright, *Human Relations and Hospital Care*, Routledge, 1964; and Enid Mills, *Living with Mental Illness*, Routledge, 1962.

[7] M. W. Susser and W. Watson, *Sociology in Medicine*, O.U.P., 1962, preface, p. vii. See also Susser in A. T. Welford *et al.*, *Society*, *op. cit.*

sidered some of the points mentioned above within a more general analysis of the functioning of the 'welfare state'.[1]

The family has received the attention of a number of sociologists. Thus Baskerville was interested in the marital and parental roles of a small sample of families in Greenwich. More specifically she studied the division of labour in the family, the attitudes and ideals of family life and the location of authority within the family.[2] Some of the studies have considered different aspects of the failures in the functioning of family life or its actual breakdown. O. R. McGregor examined the phenomenon of divorce in the light of the changing pattern of family life.[3] In A. F. Philp's study of 129 families with multiple problems an attempt was made 'to identify some of the major factors which appeared to create difficulty for these families'.[4] Although Hannah Gavron was not concerned with family failure as such in her study, she paid attention to one of the important problems facing the family in the modern urban environment. She studied the conflict situation produced by the fact that emancipated women aspire to outside roles which in some social classes become thwarted, where women with young children become housebound mothers and have to become resigned to play only the latter role.[5] The changing role of married women in industrialized society was surveyed by Viola Klein, whose interest concerned in particular women's role as employees.[6]

[1] R. M. Titmuss, *Essays on the Welfare State*, Allen & Unwin, 1958.

[2] D. R. Baskerville, 'Behaviour Patterns of Families in a London Borough: A Study of Marital and Parental Roles', unpbl. M.A. thesis, Univ. of London, 1963. Another example is Peter Townsend's study in Bethnal Green which dealt with the structure of family life in relation to old people (*The Family Life of Old People*, Routledge, 1957).

[3] O. R. McGregor, *Divorce in England*, Heinemann, 1957.

[4] A. F. Philp, *Family Failure*, Faber, 1963, p. 24.

[5] Hannah Gavron, *The Captive Wife*, Routledge, 1966.

[6] Viola Klein, *Britain's Married Women Workers*, Routledge, 1965.

It was mentioned above that Pauline Morris was interested in the effect that imprisonment of the husband has on family life. The following five specific hypotheses were tested by her: (1) 'Family relationships following upon conviction and imprisonment will follow a pattern set by family relationships which existed before imprisonment'; (2) 'Wives with wide kinship networks will seek additional support from them during the husband's imprisonment'; (3) 'Utilization of the statutory and voluntary social services will be greater and more systematic amongst the families of habitual offenders than amongst those of first offenders'; (4) 'The wives of prisoners with children of school age will seek employment; by contrast those with children under school age will not be employed, nor will those where there are children in both groups'; (5) 'The adjustment of the family to imprisonment will vary with the type of offence, and with the extent of previous criminal experience'.[1]

Ronald Fletcher tested the prevailing view that 'the contemporary family in Britain shows instability and signs of decline' by bringing together historical and contemporary material.[2] Similarly, J. A. and Olive Banks used published material to test a clearly set-up hypothesis regarding middle-class family planning in Victorian England. This was 'that as the rise of feminism coincided with the fall of the birth rate in England, the relationship between the two was a *causal* one'.[3]

Other aspects of family life, such as the effects of the neighbourhood, whether slum or suburb, on extended kin relations or social networks, have also received attention,[4] but

---

[1] Pauline Morris, *op. cit.*, pp. 23, 24.

[2] Ronald Fletcher, *The Family and Marriage*, Penguin, 1962, p. 17.

[3] J. A. and Olive Banks, *Feminism and Family Planning in Victorian England*, Liverpool U.P., 1964, p. vii; J. A. Banks, *Prosperity and Parenthood*, Routledge, 1954.

[4] See, e.g., J. M. Mogey, *Family and Neighbourhood*, O.U.P., 1956;

these studies often encompass a wider area of social relationships and in many cases are in fact community studies.

Education is a topic which has generated a tremendous amount of sociological literature. The main aspect of the enquiries in this field has been the connexion between education and social change. J. B. Mays has investigated this link in a part of central Liverpool, his particular concern being with 'how far the ideas embodied in the 1944 Act [have] been realised in the schools serving the older urban neighbourhoods'.[1] Much work has been done on the question of how education is linked to social mobility, shown in the study directed by D. V. Glass,[2] and on the relationship between social class and educational opportunity investigated by J. E. Floud, A. H. Halsey and others.[3] The link between social class and education was also basically the interest in the researches by Olive Banks, Brian Jackson and Denis Marsden. Banks examined the influence that England's educational system had on its social and occupational hierarchy. She considered the move to greater equality and set this against the persistence of social prestige attaching to the grammar school, which also plays the role of social selector.[4] Jackson, while still concerned with the problem of selection, looked farther

---

E. Bott, *Family and Social Network*, Tavistock, 1957; Madeline Kerr, *The People of Ship Street*, Routledge, 1958; M. Young and P. Willmott, *Family and Kinship in East London*, Routledge, 1957; P. Willmott and M. Young, *Family and Class in a London Suburb*, Routledge, 1960; K. Rosser and C. C. Harris, *Family and Social Change—A Study of South Wales*, Routledge, 1965.

[1] J. B. Mays, *Education and the Urban Child*, Liverpool U.P., 1962, p. 1.

[2] D. V. Glass (ed.), *Social Mobility in Britain*, Routledge, 1956; see also D. Lockwood in Welford, *op. cit.*, and 'Education and Social Mobility' in *The Listener*, 27 Oct. 1966.

[3] J. E. Floud, A. H. Halsey and F. M. Martin (eds.), *Social Class and Educational Opportunity*, Heinemann, 1957.

[4] Olive Banks, *Parity and Prestige in English Secondary Education*, Routledge, 1955.

back and studied the effect of streaming in pre-secondary education.[1] The question of the extent to which such selection, whether at the primary or secondary stage, was influenced by class factors rather than by factors of talent or ability, was investigated further by Jackson and Marsden.[2] Basil Bernstein's interest was in the interrelationship between social structure, forms of speech and the subsequent regulation of behaviour, but more specifically his enquiries revolved around 'the differential response to educational opportunity made by children from different social classes'.[3]

Continuing in the same field but dealing with higher education, we come across Peter Marris,[4] who cast the net widely in an attempt to discuss the expectations of students, their relations with the staff, the influence of different kinds of accommodation, the perception of students regarding the quality of education received and how their experience of higher education would be relevant to their role in society. Similar topics were looked at by Ferdynand Zweig.[5] Both Zweig and Marris were, however, particularly concerned with the future of this elite group of undergraduates.[6] Other writers have looked at different aspects. L. F. Douglas in a comparative study of students in the physical and social sciences was interested in the differences, if any, between these streams as regards their attitudes to university education.[7] Stephen Cotgrove examined the traditional aspects of

[1] Brian Jackson, *Streaming*, Routledge, 1964.
[2] Brian Jackson and Dennis Marsden, *Education and the Working Class*, Penguin, 1966.
[3] B. B. Bernstein, 'The Sociological Conditions and Consequences of Two Linguistic Codes: with Special Reference to Socialization', unpbl. PH.D. thesis, Univ. of London, 1963, p. 6.
[4] Peter Marris, *The Experience of Higher Education*, Routledge, 1964.
[5] Ferdynand Zweig, *The Student in the Age of Anxiety*, Heinemann, 1963.
[6] Marris, *op. cit.*, p. 153; Zweig, *op. cit.*, p. xi.
[7] L. F. Douglas, 'Types of Students and their Outlook on University Education', unpbl. PH.D. thesis, Univ. of London, 1964.

higher technical education in the light of the changing needs of an industrial society.[1]

Still concerned with education, but not linking it to social stratification or occupation as most of the above studies have done, was Joan Brothers' study in which she set out 'to show how changes in the educational system have affected religious attitudes and institutions'. More precisely, in her study she dealt with 'the consequences which current educational policy is having for the social organization of Roman Catholicism in Liverpool'.[2] And finally Raymond Williams dealt with 'education' in the broader sense of that word in his work on the present-day media of communication. He was particularly concerned with developments regarding the control of the mass media.[3]

There are two main aspects of the research that has been carried out in the field of religion. On the one hand there is a concern with the way religious institutions or groups function, i.e. their organization, and specifically their social-control functions. On the other hand there is the general question of secularization which enters into most of the literature in this field. Dealing with some of these studies we come across, for instance, Bryan Wilson's investigation of three larger sectarian organizations in contemporary Britain: 'Each is examined in terms of its teaching and practices; its organization; its self-interpretation and relation to the wider society, and the changes experienced in these regards; its social teachings and practices; its grounds and techniques of recruitment; its social class, age, sex, and educational structure.'[4] Conor Ward

[1] Stephen F. Cotgrove, *Technical Education and Social Change*, Allen & Unwin, 1958, pp. v, 202. Another study dealing with technical education is that by Marie Jahoda, *The Education of Technologists*, Tavistock, 1963.

[2] Brothers, *op. cit.*, p. 1.

[3] R. Williams, *Britain in the Sixties: Communication*, Penguin, 1962.

[4] Bryan R. Wilson, *Sects and Society—A Sociological Study of Three Religious Groups in Britain*, Heinemann, 1961, p. 6.

chose a parish which he surveyed to provide 'empirical information relating to the operation of a parochial system in a modern city'.[1] More particularly he was concerned to describe the relationship between the priest and the people on which 'much of the character of the parochial structure and the form of social relations in the parish is likely to depend'.[2] A. E. C. W. Spencer has dealt briefly with the structure and organization of the Catholic church in England.[3]

The question of secularization has been considered in one of the earlier studies by John Highet. In his study of the churches of Scotland he considered the tendency of people to show indifference to the church and the reaction of the churches to this changed situation.[4] The same themes were considered more recently by Bryan Wilson, who in a comparative study of England and America dealt with the pattern of secularization and the religious response.[5] David Martin's attention has been turned to a discussion of the very use of the concept of 'secularization'.[6]

And finally some studies dealing with minority groups in Britain have considered the role of religion in the maintenance of such groups. Thus, Zubrzycki analysed the role of the Catholic religion among the Polish group,[7] and the present

[1] Conor K. Ward, *Priests and People—A Study in the Sociology of Religion*, Liverpool U.P., 1965, p. 28.

[2] *ibid.*, p. 54.

[3] See J. D. Halloran and Joan Brothers (eds.), *Uses of Sociology*, Sheed & Ward, 1966, pp. 91–125.

[4] John Highet, *The Churches in Scotland Today*, Jackson, 1950, ch. II; see also John Highet, *The Scottish Churches*, Skeffington, 1960.

[5] Bryan R. Wilson, *Religion in Secular Society—Sociological Comment*, Watts, 1966.

[6] David Martin, 'Towards Eliminating the Concept of Secularization', in Julius Gould (ed.), *Penguin Survey of the Social Sciences 1965*, Penguin, 1965.

[7] J. Zubrzycki, *Polish Immigrants in Britain*, Nijhof, The Hague, 1956.

writer has considered the part played by Judaism in the life of Anglo-Jewish communities.[1]

A major concern of a number of sociologists has been the relationship between industrial organization at the level of the firm and the process of technical change. Thus W. H. Scott and his colleagues carried out an enquiry to 'assess how a particular structure influenced attitudes to a possible or impending change, and once a major change had been effected, to ascertain the consequent changes in structure and whether these in turn had modified attitudes to change'.[2] These researchers were hoping to find the factors which, by influencing attitudes, promoted or impeded technical change. Olive Banks followed up this enquiry with another intensive investigation in which she looked more closely at 'the experience of recent change and the way this related to the attitudes of the men who [had] been affected by it'.[3]

Another aspect of industrial sociology is that which concerns the behaviour of the worker and of management in the factory with regard to output, the relationship between the two, and the way they are influenced by outside factors. Thus T. Lupton was interested in the control over industrial workers on the shop floor. He postulated that 'there are discrepant systems of control, and discrepant role expectations associated with these' but that at the same time 'the pattern of social relationships persists and exhibits regularity'. This led him to conclude that 'there must exist some mechanisms for resolving or handling the discrepancies'. On the basis of field work in two workshops he proceeded, therefore, 'to show how

[1] E. Krausz, *op. cit.*, and E. Krausz, 'A Sociological Field Study of Jewish Suburban Life in Edgware, 1962–3, with Special Reference to Minority Identification', unpbl. PH.D. thesis, Univ. of London, 1965.

[2] W. H. Scott, J. A. Banks, A. H. Halsey, T. Lupton, *Technical Change and Industrial Relations*, Liverpool U.P., 1956, p. 6.

[3] Olive Banks, *The Attitudes of Steel Workers to Technical Change*, Liverpool U.P., 1960, p. 8.

these mechanisms operate and how behaviour is affected by them'.[1] J. A. Banks was concerned with attitudes of workers to 'participation' in the life of the firm. For this purpose he isolated and studied three aspects of the formal organization of the work: (1) the employees' positive acceptance of 'the system whereby the firm attempts to achieve its goal of efficient production'; (2) participation as revealed by the system of joint consultation; and (3) the operation of trade unionism in the firm.[2] Anne Bird concentrated her attention on management–worker conflict and was particularly interested in the patterns of dispute in the workshop.[3] The role of the foreman was studied by J. D. Mather. After a survey of existing literature this researcher formulated the hypotheses that (a) 'not all foremen have the same role to perform'; and (b) that 'these role variations can be explained by reference to a certain set of clearly defined factors'.[4] Two light engineering factories were studied in order to test these hypotheses.

Taking a more general look at the 'sociology of industry', Tom Burns distinguishes between the study of 'industrialism', categorizing thus the studies whose 'interests bear on the *external* references of the industrial system', and the study of 'industrial sociology', a category which contains research 'directed towards the *internal* order of industry'.[5] In so far as the studies considered above have been undertaken within the bounds of the firm, the factory or the workshop, although a consideration of the external influences of the wider social

[1] T. Lupton, *On the Shop Floor*, Pergamon, 1963, p. 10.

[2] J. A. Banks, *Industrial Participation*, Liverpool U.P., 1960, p. 19.

[3] Anne D. Bird, 'A Sociological Analysis of Management–Worker Conflict in Industry', unpbl. M.A. thesis, Univ. of Manchester, 1960.

[4] J. D. Mather, 'A Comparative Sociological Study of Foremen in Two Engineering Factories in North-west England', unpbl. M.A.ECON. thesis, Univ. of Manchester, 1959, pp. 1, 2.

[5] Tom Burns, 'The Sociology of Industry', in Welford, *Society*, *op. cit.*, p. 185.

structure has usually entered into these researches, they can be regarded as falling in the category of 'industrial sociology'.

Shifting attention from the firm and the workshop to occupation, we encounter a whole series of studies which have either emanated from or were clearly linked with a general framework developed by D. V. Glass and others who co-operated with him; a framework which focused on social differentiation and mobility.[1] The study of social mobility naturally implied a close investigation of the process of educational selection,[2] but here we are particularly interested in looking at the studies dealing with the development of occupational groups and their positions in a system of social stratification. In this vein R. K. Kelsall studied the higher civil servants and A. Tropp considered the professional group of elementary schoolteachers.[3] According to David Lockwood, 'Both these books were the outcome of the original research intention to concentrate on the problems of recruitment, social status and professional organization in middle-class occupations that play an important part in the national power structure or in the process of social mobility'.[4] David Lockwood himself investigated clerical workers with particular reference to their 'class consciousness'. More particularly his *leitmotif*, as he puts it, was to test the charge that the blackcoated worker had a 'false' class consciousness.[5]

[1] D. V. Glass (ed.), *Social Mobility in Britain*, Routledge, 1964.
[2] see above, pp. 28, 29.
[3] R. K. Kelsall, *The Higher Civil Servants in Britain*, Routledge, 1955; A. Tropp, *The School Teachers*, Heinemann, 1957.
[4] D. Lockwood, *The Blackcoated Worker*, Allen & Unwin, 1958, preface. There have also been other studies dealing with professions, e.g. B. A. McFarlane, 'The Chartered Engineer', unpbl. PH.D. thesis, Univ. of London, 1961; Brian Abel-Smith and Robert Stevens, *Lawyers and the Courts*, Heinemann, 1967; G. L. Millerson (see below, p. 54), dealt generally with professional associations in England and Wales.
[5] *op. cit.*, p. 13.

I. C. Cannon's work also falls in the above category. He took the skilled worker in one occupation, that of the compositor, and considered how with relatively high status, high earnings and literacy the compositor became drawn into the working-class movement. He also examined the changes occurring in certain areas of social stratification, 'in particular the effect of rising levels of living of a section of the working class on its ideology'.[1] A general study of people's attitudes to social inequality was undertaken by W. G. Runciman. One of his main aims was to find out 'what is the relation between institutionalized inequalities and the awareness or resentment of them'.[2] Ferdynand Zweig was also interested in a general way in the question of class consciousness, although he started out with the aim of studying the mutual impact of family life and industry. But although this remained his central theme he broadened his topic early on in his investigation. As he says, 'the study very soon transcended its original aim, and became a study of social change, an enquiry into working and living conditions of the industrial worker as they have been affected by post-war development'. The development Zweig investigated was one he claimed to be showing that working-class life was moving towards new middle-class values and middle-class existence.[3]

Finally it should be mentioned that some composite volumes include many studies dealing with special groups or problems. To give just one example, in *Society: Problems and Methods of Study* edited by A. T. Welford and others, there are contributions dealing, for instance, with such topics as family

[1] I. C. Cannon, 'The Social Situation of the Skilled Worker: a Study of the Compositor in London', unpbl. PH.D. thesis, Univ. of London, 1961, p. 8.

[2] W. G. Runciman, *Relative Deprivation and Social Justice*, Routledge, 1966, p. 3.

[3] F. Zweig, *op. cit.*, p. ix.

environment and mental illness or demographic aspects of an aging population.[1]

A large number of studies deal with the relations between Britain's indigenous population and the immigrants who have come to live here. Anthony Richmond reviewed the earlier studies in this category,[2] which includes the researches of M. P. Banton, K. L. Little and S. F. Collins on coloured minorities, and M. Freedman, H. Brotz and J. H. Robb on the Jewish minority. More recently a general survey of the situation, including both white and coloured minority groups, was presented by Elspeth Huxley. She wrote particularly on contemporary housing, employment and educational problems.[3] The special position of coloured immigrants was considered by J. A. G. Griffith and other writers.[4] C. E. Fiscian concentrated on the sociological and psychological aspects of anti-English prejudice among West Indians in London. The purpose of his research was to see whether findings from studies of prejudice among majority groups were at all relevant or applicable to understanding prejudice prevalent in a minority group. In this context his study also had the aim 'of investigating the pattern of the reaction of a group to its minority role'.[5]

The reaction of immigrants, or rather their adjustment to the new life, has naturally been the theme of many studies. Sheila Patterson looked at the situation of the West Indian immigrant in South London as an immigrant–host relationship, regarding colour as 'only one of a number of major factors involved in the various processes of absorption'. The

---

[1] See Part II.

[2] Anthony H. Richmond, 'Britain', in *Research on Racial Relations*, UNESCO, 1966—Richmond gives the references to the studies mentioned.

[3] Elspeth Huxley, *Back Street New Worlds*, Chatto, 1964.

[4] J. A. G. Griffith *et al.*, *Coloured Immigrants in Britain*, O.U.P., 1960.

[5] C. E. Fiscian, 'Minority Group Prejudice', unpbl. PH.D. thesis, Univ. of London, 1960, see abstract.

preliminary findings showed that the originally envisaged study in terms of white–coloured relationships would not have dealt adequately with the topic.[1] Patterson then postulated certain indices of accommodation in the various areas of association, e.g. in the economic sphere she would hope to find the immigrant workers becoming more settled in their jobs, conforming generally to the customs of British workers, joining the unions and so forth, whilst in social relationships she would expect local people to be used to the presence of coloured people. Her study could then gauge, although not very accurately, the degree of immigrant accommodation in the various areas of association.[2] A somewhat different perspective was taken by the present writer in studying the adjustment to British society of Jews in Leeds. The aim was to focus attention on the specific aspect of social control concerned with the maintenance of the minority group.[3] In that study the adjustments in the controlling mechanisms were observed. J. A. Jackson in his study of the Irish in Britain pointed out why the problems of adjustment of that group received far less attention than was the case with other immigrant groups. To quote Jackson: 'With shorter distances and no significant boundaries it has been generally assumed that the migration of Scots, Welsh or Irish people to England is merely a part of a rural–urban exodus. It is further assumed that the lack of marked distinctions, such as skin colour, between the immigrants and the host population, makes the move of the Irishman to Britain a relatively uncomplicated affair, unconnected with the classic upheavals of overseas migration.'[4] He then went on to consider the adjustments the Irishman had to make in the past and those he still has to undergo today.

[1] S. Patterson, *Dark Strangers*, Tavistock, 1963, p. xiii.
[2] *ibid.*, pp. 16, 17.
[3] Krausz, *Leeds Jewry*, *op. cit.*, pp. vi, 135.
[4] J. A. Jackson, *The Irish in Britain*, Routledge, 1963, p. xii.

The immigrant groups which have received most attention have been the West Indians and Indians. In addition to Sheila Patterson's study, a general survey of the West Indians in London has been carried out by Ruth Glass,[1] and special attention has been given to the effects of migration on their religious life by C. S. H. Hill.[2] As far as Indian immigrants are concerned, Rashmi Desai studied their general pattern of integration,[3] G. S. Aurora paid special attention to the adjustment of Indian workers to life in England,[4] and A. K. Singh surveyed the adjustment and attitudes of Indian students. As a result of pilot investigations Singh was able to set up a certain number of hypotheses which he then tested. The following were his main hypotheses: (a) 'students coming from rural, traditional, upward-mobile middle-class families sending their members for the first time for foreign education would experience greater strain and difficulties in adjustment than students coming from urban, westernized, well-established upper-class families, with a tradition of foreign education for generations'; (b) 'the students with high social need but low social skill would find more difficulties in adjustment than students with low social need but high social skill'; (c) 'the adjustment and attitudes of the students would change with their length of stay in Britain in a U-shaped curve, with a "crisis" in the middle'.[5]

In a discussion of the crisis of human relations which has been reached in the world, in one of his studies Philip Mason considered the possibility that there was some connection

---

[1] *Newcomers*, Centre for Urban Studies, Allen & Unwin, 1960.

[2] Unpbl. M.A. thesis, 'The West Indian Migrant and the Church', Univ. of London, 1964.

[3] *Indian Immigrants in Britain*, O.U.P., 1963.

[4] 'Indian Workers in England', unpbl. M.A. thesis, Univ. of London, 1960.

[5] A. K. Singh, *Indian Students in Britain*, Asia Publishing House, 1963.

between the divisions we find to exist along racial lines and class divisions. He linked the factors of race prejudice and the desire to dominate over others, and pointed to the necessity to understand clearly the basis of rule in society.[1] This leads us to other studies concerned with elites. Thus T. B. Bottomore considered closely both the theories concerning elites and empirical studies about dominant groups carried out in various countries.[2] Michael Young described the rise of a new elite, that of the meritocracy.[3] Other examples of studies of elites in Britain, but within narrower fields, are F. Musgrove's consideration of the role of white-collar and professional people in the elite groups of local communities,[4] and T. J. H. Bishop's work on the process of recruitment of the power elite from the upper status group represented by Wykehamists.[5] In a study of class relations Peter Collison dealt with an interesting phenomenon in a particular locality which as he says 'seemed to invite a field study of the relationship between the people of two [housing] estates and their attitudes to one another'.[6] This was the Cutteslowe Walls built in Oxford to separate a private housing estate composed of middle-class people and a working-class council estate. It should be mentioned here that many of the studies under different categories contain aspects relating to social class. Thus B. B. Bernstein's study of linguistic codes, the community studies of Willmott and Young, and many others could be cited.

[1] Philip Mason, *Prospero's Magic*, O.U.P., 1962.
[2] T. B. Bottomore, *Elites and Society*, Watts, 1964.
[3] Michael Young, *The Rise of the Meritocracy*, Thames & Hudson, 1958.
[4] F. Musgrove, *The Migratory Elite*, Heinemann, 1963.
[5] T. J. H. Bishop, *Winchester and the Public School Elite*, Faber, 1967.
[6] P. Collison, *The Cutteslowe Walls: A Study in Social Class*, Faber, 1963, p. 14.

THEORETICAL WORKS

Finally we shall look at the last category of studies, the theoretical works, which as we said aim at general statements regarding the processes of society and the study of social life. Morris Ginsberg's volume is one of the best examples of such a study.[1] It is true that when he deals with the ideas of progress, evolution and development his arguments and statements are philosophical. But his theories are always sociologically oriented, and his discussions of 'the comparative method' or of 'sociology as the study of the forms of association and social relations' are important and basic contributions to the theoretical aspects of the discipline. Ginsberg's work demonstrates, at any rate, the difficulty of keeping the study of society clear from other disciplines such as philosophy. Donald MacRae argues that sociology can also not be isolated from ideology and politics, even though the discipline regards ideology 'as an appropriate object of sociological study'.[2] As MacRae states, the topics dealt with in his work impinge on politics and 'can all arouse not only detached and scholarly interest, but also strong feelings and concern about policy whether in the citizen, the missionary, or the social worker'. The relationship of sociology to yet another discipline— biology—is discussed in a volume edited by Michael Banton.[3] The discussion revolves around two opposing points of view. One is that which follows Darwinism and maintains that heredity in its interaction with other factors determines the major features of social life and that, therefore, social research must start from biological principles. The other

[1] Morris Ginsberg, *Evolution and Progress: Essays in Sociology and Social Philosophy*, vol. 3, Heinemann, 1961.

[2] D. G. MacRae, *Ideology and Society*, Heinemann, 1961, p. x.

[3] Michael Banton (ed.), *Darwinism and the Study of Society: a Centenary Symposium*, Tavistock, 1961.

contends that 'social Darwinism' ignores the distinctive characteristics of human nature and returns us to 'the law of the jungle'. The uses to which a knowledge of biology can be put in sociology are then discussed.

Some writers have concerned themselves with discussing the scientific approach to sociology. Thus John Rex puts forward ideas regarding a scientific approach in sociology which emphasizes the use of theoretical models. He discusses the extent to which such models are a useful orientation to sociological research rather than constituting just 'abstract system building or armchair theorizing'.[1] John Madge in his consideration of the needs of scientific sociology stresses in particular the incompleteness of systematic theory to guide the building up of sociological knowledge. He illustrates, however, through many studies how 'the conceptual equipment brought to bear on each fresh problem is increasingly regulated by what has gone before'.[2] The possibility of a 'value free' sociology is discussed by Charles Madge, who considers the problem of developing an adequate picture of society that takes into account value itself.[3] Quentin Gibson, on the other hand, discusses the possibility of applying the logic of enquiry in the natural sciences to the social sciences (including sociology).[4] Finally, T. B. Bottomore[5] and S. Andreski[6] provide critical accounts of both theories and methods contained in sociology and pay special attention to a very wide range of social institutions in society.

[1] John Rex, *Key Problems of Sociological Theory*, Routledge, 1961, p. vii.

[2] John Madge, *The Origins of Scientific Sociology*, Tavistock, 1963, p. 1.

[3] Charles Madge, *Society in the Mind*, Faber, 1963.

[4] Quentin Gibson, *The Logic of Social Enquiry*, Routledge, 1960.

[5] Bottomore, *Sociology*, *op. cit.*

[6] Andreski, *Elements of Comparative Sociology*, *op. cit.*

GENERAL COMMENTS

The wide range of topics mentioned suggests that sociological research now covers most of the areas of social life. It is also evident that most of the studies are problem-oriented. It is not difficult to see that real problems can be the best stimulators of research. The problem area appears as a field highlighted for study; and the researcher may be strongly motivated by a wish to solve the problem and thus prove the practical uses of his discipline. The implications for sociological research are manifold. Problem orientation need not, but may, add to the danger of insufficient detachment in the researcher. The fact that complete detachment might be an unattainable ideal[1] does not deny the possibility that problem-oriented research may be fraught more seriously with the danger of involvement and bias. D. G. MacRae's stricture that too much problem-oriented research might prevent the development of sociology as an intellectual discipline[2] appears, however, somewhat severe. But it is true that some of the literature in certain problem areas, such as education, race relations or juvenile delinquency, appears to have been more concerned with the topicality of the problem than with advancing sociological research as such through the use of more sophisticated methods and techniques. Similarly, there is some danger in the claim that the research of the social scientist must be 'field determined', i.e. guided by the needs experienced in practical life, which would mean 'beginning with practice, however imperfect scientifically, and working back to theory and more systematic research that may test this'.[3] Practical requirements may simply lead

[1] See above, p. 8.

[2] D. G. MacRae, 'The Crisis in Sociology', in J. H. Plumb (ed.), *Crisis in the Humanities*, Penguin, 1964, pp. 134, 135.

[3] See *Social Research and a National Policy for Science*, paper of the Council of the Tavistock Institute of Human Relations, Tavistock Pamphlet no. 7, 1964, p. 5.

to sociologically superficial 'market research' type of studies and reports which might never elicit further theoretically oriented and more rigorously executed research. Michael Young's plea for 'innovation research' may resolve the difficulties. For whilst this kind of approach, where innovation and research are linked,[1] can focus on problems, it can at the same time be more advanced methodologically by introducing and encouraging research through experiments. It is true that the problem of involvement still remains, but this is a general problem that the sociologist must face.[2]

Norbert Elias has elaborated on this problem, the reason for its existence, as he says, being the fact that the sociologist is himself involved in the phenomena he studies, a condition which is, however, necessary for his understanding of the phenomena. He warns against the acceptance of models from other sciences dealing with less complex systems, a procedure which in his view simply leads to 'a kind of pseudo-detachment'. Apart from the need to have suitable models[3] the difficulty is that of attaining sufficient scientific autonomy. In Elias' words: 'The problem confronting those who study one or the other aspects of human groups is how to keep their two roles as participant and as inquirer clearly and consistently apart and, as a professional group, to establish in their work the undisputed dominance of the latter.'[4] The only comment possible here is a rather negative one. Apart from 'problem-orientation' as an influencing factor, the degree or kind of involvement present when selecting topics or areas of research is not clearly discernible from the foregoing account, and this is particularly true with regard to the manner in which

[1] Michael Young, *Innovation and Research in Education*, Routledge, 1965, esp. ch. 1.
[2] See above, p. 8.
[3] This point is also discussed above, p. 9.
[4] N. Elias, 'Problems of Involvement and Detachment', *British Journal of Sociology*, vol. 7, 1956, p. 238.

hypotheses were formulated. It would have been necessary, for instance, to delve into the possible alternative formulations of hypotheses in order to be able to evaluate this field properly. This is beyond the scope of this review and deserves a specialized study in its own right.

Our survey of the research carried out suggests that in some areas there is a good deal of repetition or overlap. Several investigations in the same field could be an advantage, but only if studies in particular areas were linked and hypotheses re-tested. It is desirable to replicate certain studies even in non-experimental research, a category into which most sociological work falls, for this aids the verification of past research. But the process of replication is not to be confused with mere repetition. Few examples can be given of replication, although Earl Hopper's study in the field of industrial sociology was such an exercise.[1] What we have had far too frequently, however, has been repetition, which merely leads to the dissipation of research energy and resources. To aggravate the situation many of the studies 'talked around' a topic without clearly setting up and focusing on hypotheses. Since general descriptive material is itself necessary to promote the creation of hypotheses,[2] the generality of some pieces of research may not eliminate their usefulness. However, vagueness and prolixity are to be deplored in sociological research, particularly since the subject often demands fairly extensive descriptive writing. To allow replication in research not only must hypotheses be clearly postulated but the studies in particular areas must be linked through the use of general frameworks. We found such requirements satisfied in some

[1] Under controlled structural conditions in an English factory, an American investigation of certain effects of supervisory styles was replicated: see Earl Hopper, 'Some Effects of Supervisory Styles', *British Journal of Sociology*, vol. 16, no. 3, Sept. 1965, p. 189.

[2] See Maurice Duverger, *Introduction to the Social Sciences*, Allen & Unwin, 1964, p. 24ff.

areas, e.g. community studies and studies of social mobility, but in many areas of research, although certain individual studies had clearly set out aims, most of them added in an unclear and variegated manner to a mass of material only loosely connected. The obvious course is to have properly planned programmes to encompass a whole series of research projects and to ensure continuity and cumulativeness.[1] This is an urgent necessity if sociology is to make further advances.

[1] See below, pp. 187-98 and 207, 208.

3. Methods and techniques

Here we shall concern ourselves with the two major requirements for carrying out research. In the first place consideration
will be given to the methods used. In other words we shall
look at the fundamental orientations of the researchers, their
frames of reference and models, and the concepts and terminology resorted to.[1] We are interested in these in the sense in
which they serve as heuristic devices. To show this, examples
from the studies reviewed will be given. Secondly, again
through examples, an appraisal of the techniques or tools
through which the actual researches were carried out will be
attempted.

General approach

In so far as the general approach is concerned, it has often
been found that the historical method has been used in
combination with some other methods such as the comparative or functionalist. The former often serves as a kind of
anchorage or background against which the research into the
contemporary phenomenon can proceed. Thus I. C. Cannon
in studying the social situation of one type of skilled worker

[1] For further references regarding theoretical approach, models, frames
of reference, concepts, and terms, see esp. Llewellyn Gross (ed.), *Symposium on Sociological Theory*, Harper, New York, 1959, ch. 2 by Don
Martindale, 3 by R. Bendix and B. Berger, and 4 by R. Bierstedt;
A Dictionary of the Social Sciences, op. cit., pp. 120, 275 and 435; P.
Cohen, 'Models', *British Journal of Sociology*, vol. 8, no. 1, March 1966,
p. 70ff; Julius Gould,'The Vocabulary of Sociology', *ibid.*, vol. 14, no.
1, p. 29ff; and W. J. H. Sprott, *Sociology at the Seven Dials, op. cit.*

provides first an historical account, and then through the functionalist approach considers firstly the relationship between the social condition of members in the given occupation and their class and political identification, and then the influence that the occupation itself had on these identifications.[1] Ronald Fletcher, similarly, in considering the family and marriage in Britain of the 1960s in the historical context, uses a functionalist approach in that he focuses attention on the functions of the family today and compares them with its functions at an earlier period.[2] The same is true of the work of T. J. H. Bishop, who traces the success of a century of Winchester College pupils and then goes on to consider the functions of this public school in the system of social stratification in Britain.[3] F. Musgrove's framework in his study of the migratory elite can also be regarded as functionalist-historical, for he considers the movements of elites from the aspect of the interconnectedness between institutions such as the educational system on the one hand and the economic aspects of urbanization on the other. He considers this relationship in the historical setting of the socio-economic changes since the industrial revolution.[4]

Several more examples can be given to show that the functionalist approach is often used together with historical studies, which on the whole facilitates a demonstration of the social change overtaking an institution or a whole society. Such a combined approach, however, also implies the use of the comparative method in the sense that the characteristics and functioning of an institution or society are compared at

[1] I. C. Cannon, 'The Social Situation of the Skilled Worker: a Study of the Compositor in London', unpbl. ph.D. thesis, Univ. of London, 1961, p. 9.

[2] R. Fletcher, *Britain in the Sixties: Family and Marriage*, Penguin, 1962, p. 177.

[3] T. J. H. Bishop, *Winchester and the Public School Elite*, Faber, 1967.

[4] F. Musgrove, *The Migratory Elite*, Heinemann, 1963.

different points in time. Joan Brothers, for instance, was interested in the interaction between educational and religious institutions in Liverpool[1] and emphasised how the old devotion to the parochial setting has given way among young people to a more abstract concept of the Church.[2] The present writer in a study of Jews in Leeds has similarly attempted to show the kind of changes which have taken place in religious identification since the inception of the community. The working of social-control mechanisms in the contemporary community was compared with what was effective more than half a century earlier among the immigrant generation.[3]

But whilst comparative work is undoubtedly involved in the kind of studies mentioned so far, some studies have focused more clearly on the comparative aspect. Thus, Peter Collison in his study of the relationship between people on two adjoining housing estates in Oxford, which were of different class composition, was able to compare such relationship before and after the symbol of segregation, in the form of the Cutteslowe Walls, was removed.[4] In a series of studies carried out by Michael Young and Peter Willmott for the Institute of Community Studies the comparative approach was used specifically to investigate patterns of kinship and social class in the East End of London and a suburb on the outskirts of the metropolis.[5]

It appears that most studies, in their general approach, use some combination of the historical, functionalist and com-

---

[1] Joan Brothers, *Church and School, A Study of the Impact of Education on Religion*, Liverpool U.P., 1964.

[2] *ibid.*, p. 159.

[3] E. Krausz, *Leeds Jewry*, Heffer, Cambridge, 1964.

[4] Peter Collison, *The Cutteslowe Walls*, Faber, 1963.

[5] Willmott and Young, *Family and Class in a London Suburb*, Routledge, 1960. Other studies in addition to those mentioned above have also been found to be functionalist in their approach. See, for example, C. Vereker and J. B. Mays, *Urban Redevelopment and Social Change*, Liverpool U.P., 1961, pp. 118-9.

parative methods. One could not, therefore, agree with T. B. Bottomore that the functionalist approach has outlived its usefulness.[1] Only in its more extreme organistic formulations and in its neglect of the importance of social change can the approach be misleading.[2] Similarly the historical method must be qualified and hedged in primarily when it makes evolutionist claims or diverts attention from sociological study in favour of an historically oriented investigation. One would, on the other hand, agree with Bottomore regarding the importance of the comparative method. The situation is probably best summed up by Ely Chinoy in the following paragraph:

'The contrast between the functional and historical approaches is itself in all likelihood merely a phase in the history of sociology. If this now barely maturing discipline is to achieve its goals and fulfil its youthful hopes, these approaches . . . must be brought together into a unified whole. Already they share several common perspectives. They both entail an awareness of the complex interrelationships which exist within society and of the limitations of any simplified one-factor interpretation of social behaviour. They are both concerned with generalization rather than with the individual and the unique, and they utilize similar concepts for catching the recurrent aspects of social life. Finally, they both recognize the importance and value of a comparative approach, for whatever the problems selected for study the systematic comparison of different societies, past and present, provides both the basis for suggestive hypotheses and the material for testing them.'[3]

Models, concepts and terminology
Let us now consider the various specific models used in

[1] T. B. Bottomore, *Sociology*, Allen & Unwin, 1964, p. 54.
[2] See below, p. 18of.
[3] Ely Chinoy, *Society*: *An Introduction to Sociology*, Random House, New York, 1965, p. 77.

British sociological research. In a study of the impact of newcomers and the new industry to which they were attached, in a small traditional community, Margaret Stacey used the conflict model. Thus she says that 'when the study was first planned attention was focused on the distinction between Banburians and immigrants. It seemed likely that there were important tensions between the two groups, even that the division might be the key to the social structure of the town.'[1] Sheila Patterson in her study of West Indians in south London relies basically on the cyclical model developed by Park and Burgess. This postulates four basic processes of social interaction: competition, conflict, accommodation and assimilation.[2] Patterson describes and analyses, in particular, the processes of accommodation, but mentions also areas of competition and conflict and her scheme falls within the cyclical model.[3] F. Musgrove uses Pareto's 'circulation of elites' model when investigating the leadership in the voluntary organizations and the official bureaucracies in the towns and cities of England.[4]

Norbert Elias and John Rex have both tackled the important question of what kinds of model can most usefully be applied in empirical research. Rex compared the pluralistic model of society, which starts out with the assumption that conflict is endemic in social life, with the integrationist model, which assumes the prevalence of consensus and complete institutionalization of social relationships. Rex stressed that the pluralistic model may be more fruitful for research in some societies than others but on the whole claims that 'The model of plural society, when its workings are more fully understood,

---

[1] Margaret Stacey, *Tradition and Change: A Study of Banbury*, O.U.P., 1960, p. 165.

[2] R. E. Park and E. W. Burgess, *Introduction to the Science of Sociology*, Univ. of Chicago Press, 1921, chs. 8–11.

[3] Sheila Patterson, *Dark Strangers*, Tavistock, 1963, esp. p. 16.

[4] F. Musgrove, *The Migratory Elite*, *op. cit.*, pp. 12, 70.

is one which is just as essential to the sociologist as is, say, Parsons' model of an integrated social system'.[1] Elias was also concerned with finding the model that would most readily fit the realities of society. He contrasted, therefore, the sort of model which suits the physical sciences rather well, with that which must be adopted in the study of society, and noted that the model employed would also largely determine the sort of technique employed, such as the use of measuring devices and quantification. He places the different types of model on a continuum and in fact appears to regard these as themselves components of a larger model. This continuum is bounded at one of the poles by a model based on a paradigm of loosely composed units and a low degree of interdependence, and at the other pole by a model of a highly complex system which consists of 'a hierarchy of inter-locking part systems and part processes and whose constituents are inter-dependent to such an extent that they cannot be isolated from their unit without radical changes in their properties as well as in those of the unit itself'.[2] Although Elias does not think that the latter model will have universal applicability to sociological problems, he tends to regard it as the one more in line with the nature of the subject matter with which sociology is mostly concerned.[3]

The above examples will suffice to show the kind of models used in research work. Not all studies state explicitly the models they employ, but where they are analytical rather than

[1] John Rex, 'The Plural Society in Sociological Theory', *British Journal of Sociology*, vol. 10, no. 2, June 1959, p. 124.

[2] Norbert Elias, 'Problems of Involvement and Detachment', *British Journal of Sociology*, vol. 7, 1956, p. 243.

[3] Elias says that between the two poles would be spaced out 'intermediary models graded according to the degree of differentiation and integration of their constituents'. He also stresses that not all physical problems fit the 'congeries' model and not all sociological problems fit the 'system' model. See *ibid.*, p. 243, esp. n. 1.

descriptive, models are invariably used. This is natural, for as Percy Cohen says 'almost all sociological analysis does involve the implicit use of models'.[1] For one is bound to have some pattern in one's mind regarding the society, group or social phenomenon one investigates. It is true that the use of such models influences the sociologist's observations as well as his analysis of the observed or readily available facts—it thus shapes his research. Yet it is obvious, as Inkeles says, that for sociological, as for any scientific work, the use of models is indispensable.[2]

Finally we shall look at some of the concepts which British sociologists have been employing. Thus T. J. H. Bishop has relied on a somewhat modified Weberian concept of social stratification using a threefold scale in terms of wealth, authority and status.[3] Similarly James Littlejohn relied on Weber's concept of status groups in his investigation of social stratification in a rural parish.[4] F. Musgrove, in considering the position of youth in the modern society of Britain, employs the concepts of 'status' and 'role'.[5] And again the concept of 'role' is used in studying the domestic and social consequences of married women who are working.[6]

Michael Banton draws attention to the overall importance of the concept of 'role', for 'it can be widely applied in the analysis of social systems',[7] whether simple or complex.

[1] Percy S. Cohen, 'Models', *British Journal of Sociology*, vol. 18, no. 1, March 1966, p. 70.

[2] Alex Inkeles, *What is Sociology?*, Prentice-Hall, Englewood Cliffs, New Jersey, 1964, p. 28. For a definition of 'model' see E. A. Gellner in *Dictionary of the Social Sciences*, *op. cit.*, p. 435. For a discussion of 'concept' see Gellner, *ibid.*, p. 120.

[3] T. J. H. Bishop, *op. cit.*

[4] James Littlejohn, *Westrigg*, Routledge, 1963, p. 76.

[5] F. Musgrove, *Youth and the Social Order*, Routledge, 1964, pp. 1, 110.

[6] Caroline R. Hutton, 'Married Women on Full-time Shift Work', unpbl. M.A. thesis, Univ. of London, 1962.

[7] M. Banton, *Roles*, Tavistock, 1965, p. 18.

The advantage of the concept is that one is familiar with the idea of having to play parts in social life. Banton goes on to show how with the 'role' concept we can construct a representation of social organization and the kind of analysis of society to which this can lead. Elizabeth Bott used the concept of 'social network' in studying the external social relationships of families.[1] J. A. and Olive Banks use the concept of 'feminism' in their investigation of the relationship between women's emancipation and the fall in birth rate.[2] The present writer in his study of the Jewish minority uses the concepts of 'acculturation' and 'assimilation'.[3] The concept of 'reference group' is used by W. G. Runciman to explain attitudes to social inequality.[4] And to mention just one more concept introduced more recently, Charles Madge talks of 'social eidos' as meaning 'the predominant character of the whole stock of ideas available in a society or group'.[5]

Concepts, according to Gellner, 'may be seen as the meanings of terms', and 'discussions of concepts in the social sciences tend to be a matter of the choice of terms and, more importantly, of their definitions'.[6] One of the main problems encountered, as Gould points out, is 'the overlap between general and scientific usage' of many of the terms in the vocabulary of sociology.[7] Other disciplines, too, have to

[1] Elizabeth Bott, *Family and Social Network*, Tavistock, 1957, pp. 58, 216ff.

[2] *op. cit.*

[3] *op. cit.*, pp. 135–7. See also, e.g., the use of the concept 'assimilation' in a study by C. S. H. Hill, 'The West Indian Migrant and the Church', unpbl. M.A. thesis, Univ. of London, 1964.

[4] W. G. Runciman, *Relative Deprivation and Social Justice*, Routledge, 1966, ch. 2.

[5] C. Madge, *Society in the Mind*, Faber, 1964, p. 13.

[6] E. A. Gellner, in *Dictionary of the Social Sciences*, *op. cit.*, pp. 120–1.

[7] Julius Gould, 'The Vocabulary of Sociology', *British Journal of Sociology*, vol. 14, no. 1, March 1963, p. 33.

face this problem. Harold Merskey makes the point clearly so far as psychiatry is concerned: 'Terms are often used in psychiatry which have a different meaning in ordinary speech. This is probably unavoidable since, even if such terms were not taken from the vernacular into psychiatry, the reverse process would be certain to occur.'[1] In sociology, as in other disciplines, in order to overcome confusion, careful and specialized definitions must be given to terms used. To illustrate, one can quote, for example, the special meaning with which the term 'culture' may be invested. This comes out in Alan Little's study of Borstal life where 'culture' is taken to mean the code of behaviour found in the institution among the inmates.[2] In a similar sense D. M. Downes discusses the term 'delinquent sub-culture'.[3] With certain popularly accepted terms difficulty arises because of the special meanings attached to the term by different disciplines. A case in point is 'white-collar crime', where there is disagreement in the legal and sociological views of the term. G. E. Levens, therefore, explains that as a sociologist he is not interested in the aetiology of the crime but rather in the effects of conviction. His exclusive criterion is the social status of the offender and not the particular nature of the offence. He, therefore, replaces the term 'white-collar criminal' with that of 'middle-class offender'.[4] G. L. Millerson in his work on the professional associations in England and Wales goes to great lengths to point out the difficulties regarding the use of

[1] H. Merskey and W. L. Tong, *Psychiatric Illness*, Baillière, Tindall & Cox, 1965, p. 14.

[2] A. N. Little, 'Borstal: a Study of Inmates' Attitudes to the Staff and the System', unpbl. PH.D. thesis, Univ. of London, 1961, p. 172.

[3] D. M. Downes, 'Delinquent Sub-Cultures in East London', unpbl. PH.D. thesis, Univ. of London, 1964, ch. 1.

[4] G. E. Levens, 'A Study of the Occupational and Social Mobility of "White-collar Criminals" after Discharge from Prison', unpbl. M.SC. thesis, Univ. of London, 1964, p. 14.

the term 'profession'.[1] Among various factors creating such difficulties are the semantic confusion leading to the use of this term synonymously with such words as 'occupation' or 'job', and the traditional image that has grown up around the word 'profession'. Millerson gives his own definition in order to make the term scientifically useful in his study. His definition observes the following principles: (a) high-grade, non-manual occupation; (b) designation 'profession' is not a permanent monopoly of a few occupations; (c) professional status is of dynamic quality, i.e. content may change; (d) an organized occupation is not necessarily a profession; (e) the presence, or absence, of a code of professional conduct does not signify professional or non-professional status; (f) to achieve a professional status there must be a subjective and objective recognition of the occupation as a profession.[2]

Looking at yet another term we come across the present writer's definition of a 'minority' as a group whose members identify with a specific culture distinct from that of the general population or larger society in which the group is found.[3] The term 'minority' has mostly been defined more specifically by the application of ethnic, religious or racial criteria.[4] Once again in this way an ordinary word acquires a narrower sociological meaning. In some studies, however, deviation from general dominant norms in a society has also been regarded as a valid criterion.[5] Consequently the label 'minority' has been attached to homosexuals as well as immigrants,

[1] G. L. Millerson, *The Qualifying Associations*, Routledge, 1964, p. 1ff.

[2] *ibid.*, p. 9.

[3] *op. cit.*, esp. pp. 74 and 106.

[4] See a discussion of possible definitions by Preston Valien in *Dictionary of the Social Sciences*, *op. cit.*, p. 432ff. See also R. Glass, 'Insiders-Outsiders: the Position of Minorities', *Transactions of the Fifth World Congress of Sociology*, vol. 8, International Sociological Association, 1964.

[5] See, e.g., Gordon Westwood, *A Minority: Report on the Life of the Male Homosexual in Great Britain*, Longmans, 1960.

for instance. Recently an even looser use of the term has appeared, in that 'minority' has been used simply to denote a smaller category of more isolated and more lonely old people.[1] Extending the usage of a term in this way is bound to lead to vagueness and to destroy the attempt to clarify sociological terminology.

Another instance of an ordinary word acquiring a specific meaning is 'communication', by which Raymond Williams means 'the institutions and forms in which ideas, information, and attitudes are transmitted and received'.[2] And finally it is most instructive to consider some terminological definitions made by David Martin in his study of the ideology of pacifism.[3] In it he distinguishes clearly between church, denomination and sect, and goes on to define them. Thus, for instance, he regards 'sect' as essentially a vehicle of social conflict.[4] It is important to note that in his more elaborate explanation of his definition, he applies the term equally to religious and political groups. But this further involves Martin in the need to define the very terms of 'religion' and 'political'. He draws attention to two possible types of definition: the analytic, which conceives religion as related to the universal and politics to the particular; secondly, the identification in terms of historical usage. But in so far as the existence of sects is concerned Martin argues that the two spheres are unified. Furthermore the definitional problem, he says, shows the fundamental artificiality of attempting to separate the two

[1] See Jeremy Tunstall, *Old and Alone: A Sociological Study of Old People*, Routledge, 1966, p. 3. See also Gordon F. Streib, 'Are the Aged a Minority Group?', in A. W. Gouldner and S. M. Miller (eds.), *Applied Sociology*, Free Press, Glencoe, Illinois, 1965, p. 311ff.

[2] Raymond Williams, *Britain in the Sixties: Communication*, Penguin, 1962, p. 9.

[3] D. A. Martin, 'A Study of the Ideology of Pacifism and its Background, with Special Reference to Britain 1915–1945', Ph.D. thesis, Univ. of London, 1964; and see D. A. Martin, *Pacifism*, Routledge, 1965.

[4] *ibid.*, thesis, pp. 14 and 382ff.

spheres.[1] The above examples illustrate the great care which is necessary, and the often intricate problems which arise, in connexion with the sociologist's use of terms in his research work.

TECHNIQUES

The definitions of terms, the use of concepts and models, and the adoption of some general method, are a few of the important tasks of the researcher. We shall now turn to a consideration of some of his other manifold tasks, i.e. the employment of different kinds of tools or techniques in sociological research. These can be regarded as falling into three broad categories: those belonging to the preparatory stage; those concerned with the accumulation of material; and the techniques with the aid of which the analysis and interpretation can be carried out.

The preparatory stage

The foremost technique in the preparatory stage is the pilot study. This is particularly the case where the survey is used. C. A. Moser distinguishes clearly between pre-tests and pilot studies. He makes the point that in addition to the seeking of the advice of experts and the study of the background literature on the topic of interest, pre-tests are of real importance. The pre-tests are less formalized smaller probings, e.g. 'doing a few test interviews or sending out trial forms', and they are concerned with isolated problems of the survey design; the pilot study on the other hand is 'a small-scale replica of the main survey'.[2]

Examples taken from the studies under review here show how these preparatory steps were taken in practice. Pearl

[1] *ibid.*, pp. 2, 15, 16.
[2] C. A. Moser, *Survey Methods in Social Investigation*, Heinemann, 1958, p. 44.

Jephcott's survey of slum conditions in Notting Hill started with four months spent in consulting some 60 people in official positions. They were very useful in delineating the main problems of the borough and in putting the researcher into contact with her future respondents.[1] In the field of rural sociology W. M. Williams used a pilot survey to choose the most suitable community out of four possibilities, for the purpose of studying the effects of rural depopulation on family and kinship.[2]

As far as 'pre-testing' and 'piloting' are concerned, in some studies the difference between the two does not appear clearly. Thus Gordon Westwood in his study of homosexuals mentions how the interview schedule was *pre-tested* during a *pilot survey*.[3] Again Ferdynand Zweig in his study of industrial life and its relationship to family life had a *pilot enquiry* undertaken in a Sheffield factory, which was 'based on open and informal interviews with the employees'. For the enquiries proper, however, standardized schedules were used.[4] In Alan Little's study of life in a Borstal, the stages of pre-test and piloting were more clearly differentiated. The first was 'the culture case study' used 'to sensitize the field worker to the type of problems likely to be encountered'. The piloting stage was used to try out the questionnaire and it also helped to work out the right kind of approach for allaying the fears of the inmates and staff.[5]

The pilot study is not exclusive to 'field research', although it is much more common in the latter. Thus David Martin has used it to advantage in 'library research'. Before discussing

---

[1] Pearl Jephcott, *A Troubled Area: Notes on Notting Hill*, Faber, 1964, p. 35ff.

[2] W. M. Williams, *A West Country Village: Ashworthy*, Routledge, 1963, pp. xiii–xiv.

[3] Westwood, *op. cit.*, p. 2.

[4] F. Zweig, *The Worker in an Affluent Society*, Heinemann, 1961.

[5] Little, *op. cit.*, pp. 100, 112, 122.

the development of pacifist ideology in modern Britain, he conducted a pilot study into the influence of apocalypticism in the period of the English Civil War.[1]

It is important to note that some studies in their entirety are regarded as basically pilot studies opening up the way for further, more sophisticated enquiries. The pilot survey helps, therefore, to set up the hypotheses to be tested in subsequent research. Thus D. R. Baskerville makes it clear that her study of the behaviour pattern of 40 families in Greenwich was in the nature of a pilot study. The latter suggested three areas of possible further investigation: the development of a satisfactory scale for measuring household tasks and decisions; a study of the current trend to cooperative family activity and home-centredness; and a study of the apparent ease with which middle-class families make new social contacts on new estates.[2] Similarly Joan Brothers regarded her study of the impact of education on religion as exploratory. Hence, she says, her conclusions are tentative. The function of the study was 'not to produce final conclusions but to probe promising areas'.[3]

The preparatory stage also necessarily includes the design of the research. The existing background material and pointers from pilot enquiries, the nature of the topic investigated, and the kind of financial and other help available will be the factors determining the design adopted. Two chief characteristics of the sociological field will, however, largely predetermine the basic aspects of the design. One flows from the fact that sociology deals with phenomena which are usually complex, involving a large number of highly interdependent factors. This would normally call for a matrix with a large number of

[1] *op. cit.*, pp. 100, 125.
[2] D. R. Baskerville, 'Behaviour Patterns of Families in a London Borough: a Study of Marital and Parental Roles', unpbl. M.A. thesis, Univ. of London, 1963, pp. 1, 2.
[3] *op. cit.*, p. 19.

cells, the latter to be filled by sufficient units in order to facilitate the vast number of combinations through which cross-relationships or the interdependence of the factors can be analysed. The other characteristic stems from the fact that it is seldom possible to stage experiments in connection with the study of society. In fact the research designs of most of the studies we are considering are of the non-experimental kind. We have, however, some examples of studies with experimental designs, most of which are of the *before-after/ without control groups* type. The studies which used follow-up surveys, to be mentioned below when discussing the techniques employed to accumulate data, have basically this design. A very good example is Peter Collison's before/after surveys in the Cutteslowe study, where he did not employ any control groups.[1] The absence of control groups is a drawback which often may not be possible to avoid. G. Westwood, for instance, dropped the idea of having a control group when his pilot study showed the very wide difference in behaviour among homosexuals.[2]

It is of interest to reproduce here in some detail the reasons for the abandonment of the idea of using control groups where an attempt had in fact been made to obtain such groups. Pauline Morris, who undertook a study of the problems of prisoners' families, relates how initially it was decided to obtain a control group by selecting 'a group of families in which the husband was under social stigma as a result of conflict with the law, but had been placed on probation and where there was no question of separation. It was intended that the nature of the offence be such that it seemed likely that, had he received a sentence of imprisonment, it would have been for approximately eighteen months to two years.'[3]

---

[1] *op. cit.*, appendix A and pp. 174-6.

[2] *op. cit.*, p. 194.

[3] Pauline Morris, for P.E.P., *Prisoners and their Families*, Allen & Unwin, 1965, p. 30.

Arrangements were made with the Home Office and the Probation Service, who were willing to cooperate. But the following difficulties were encountered: (1) Probation records varied considerably. To rectify this, many additional interviews would have had to be carried out, for which there were no resources; (2) Attendance at some of the hearings revealed that it would have been unrealistic to predict whether a man might have got a sentence of the duration mentioned above. It also appeared that most of those put on probation were unmarried and this placed a severe limitation on the selection of cases; (3) It was hoped that the information required would be automatically covered in the course of the normal work of Probation Officers. This was not so, and consequently the additional work that Probation Officers might have been put to would have been burdensome. For these reasons it was decided to give up the attempt to use control groups. It is somewhat surprising, however, to find that Pauline Morris gives the additional reason that 'since it was a comparative group of doubtful validity in the first place, this part of the research was abandoned'. In that case why was the attempt made at all?

Although difficulties were encountered in obtaining control groups in a study of homosexuality carried out by Michael Schofield, the latter, unlike Westwood, did use such groups for two of the three types of homosexuals he studied. Thus a group of homosexual patients were seen first, and subsequently a group of non-homosexual patients under psychiatric treatment was obtained to match the homosexual patients by age and education. The two groups were not matched by occupation but the results showed that they were not dissimilar in this respect. The prime difficulties in matching arose, however, when the reasons why homosexual patients sought psychiatric treatment were considered, and when it became evident that classifications into degrees of sickness could be established for neither group. For these reasons, Schofield says, comparisons can only be made with caution.[1] For a group of homosexuals who had not received treatment and who had not been convicted of homosexual offences, similarly a group of non-homosexuals to match for age and education was obtained. The main difficulty here was to explain to the latter group the importance of control groups. Thus Schofield says that initially cooperation could be gained, but that 'as soon as the idea of the control group is explained, this seems to cause a deterioration in response. It is almost as we have said: We are not really interested in you; there is something much more important that concerns us; you are being used as a kind of measuring stick. People are not flattered by this explanation after they have gone to some trouble to cooperate.'[2] Finally no control group was obtained for the group of homosexuals who were convicted and who were inmates of prisons; 'The Prison Commissioners would not agree to prisoners other than those convicted of homosexual offences being questioned about sexual matters'.[3]

Controlling at least for some important variables, which is not the same as the proper and full use of control groups, takes an essential part in some studies. B. B. Bernstein, in connection with a study of linguistic orientation, when presenting differences in the IQ profile of groups of different social-class composition, controlled for age by matching his middle- and working-class subjects in regard to this variable.[4]

It must be remembered that the research design ultimately determines the kind of analysis which it will be possible to apply. Thus, special steps have to be taken when designing

[1] Michael Schofield, *Sociological Aspects of Homosexuality*, Longmans, 1965, p. 218.
[2] *ibid.*, p. 220.
[3] *ibid.*, p. 3.
[4] B. B. Bernstein, *op. cit.* (see above, p. 29), p. 4; another example of matching samples, this time in respect of income and social status, is found in H. E. Bracey, *Neighbours*, Routledge, 1964.

a research project to enable the use of attitude scales. Such scales have been used in several studies, one example being F. Musgrove's work on the status of youth in our society.[1] Similarly the designs must be appropriate for the application of factor analysis or multivariate analysis, as in L. F. Douglas' study of students,[2] and in Moser and Scott's study of characteristics of towns,[3] respectively.

Finally where, for instance, the design provides for the random selection of a sample and ensures an adequate sample size, the meaningful use of statistical tests of significance becomes possible, a good example being the Willmott and Young study of *Family and Class in a London Suburb*.[4] We shall return later to a discussion of some of these analytical tools, and their place in sociological research in Britain.

Getting the facts

Once the researcher has obtained the necessary 'leads' and guiding lights, through pre-tests or pilot studies or at least a thorough acquaintanceship with the background to the field and specific topic he is about to investigate, and once he has decided on the research design, his attention turns to the major task of gathering the raw material upon which his study will be based. It must be understood that whilst he may have decided earlier on the methods to be used and hypotheses to be tested[5] these may be modified in the light

[1] F. Musgrove, *Youth and the Social Order*, Routledge, 1964, pp. 11, 12, 90, etc.

[2] L. F. Douglas, 'Types of Students and their Outlook on University Education', unpbl. PH.D. thesis, Univ. of London, 1964, p. 158.

[3] C. A. Moser and Wolf Scott, *British Towns*, Oliver & Boyd, 1961, p. 66.

[4] *op. cit.*, pp. x, 133, 172.

[5] Decisions, prior to pilot studies, regarding methods and hypotheses are usually arrived at through hints gained from other similar studies or general texts on theories and methods of sociology. But this in itself can be regarded as just another aspect of the preparatory stage.

of the findings of pilot studies. He may even abandon the idea of studying the problem he set out originally to investigate, or the focus of attention may shift as a result of preliminary findings or hunches. We have already dealt with the kind of problems investigated and, in particular, the hypotheses set up and tested. Bearing in mind, therefore, the dual role of the preparatory stage in giving a basic guide regarding the hypotheses which are to be tested, as well as throwing light on the best techniques to be used, we shall now turn our attention solely to these techniques.

The main dichotomy which suggests itself is between those studies which rely primarily on secondary material and those which base themselves on a combination of such secondary data and first-hand information collected expressly for the purposes of the study, or in fact rely entirely on such 'primary data'. From the standpoint of the quality and usefulness of the results of a piece of research, there is intrinsically no superiority that could be attached to either of the ways in which the necessary information is obtained. The research based on secondary material may produce a brilliant analysis of a problem whilst the 'primary data' might result in meaningless generalizations, or vice versa. There is also no premium to be put on the material being collected specially for or by sociologists. Incidental and indirect information may be most useful for sociological enquiry. But when material is collected specifically for such research, this may allow greater ease for manipulation of both design and analysis, and getting such primary data would, therefore, be to the researcher's advantage. But the kind of data one uses is often dictated by the topic chosen. A comparative study spanning a long period of several centuries must perforce rely mainly on secondary data; contemporary topics, however, can be dealt with through either primary or secondary data or a combination of these.

A few examples will suffice to illustrate the dichotomy. In the category into which studies based on 'secondary material' fall, we find books which are the result of previously published papers and which deal with a variety of issues concerning the study of society. Among these are such works as *Evolution and Progress* by Morris Ginsberg, *Sociology at the Crossroads* by T. H. Marshall and *Ideology and Society* by Donald MacRae. Again, there are those collections of papers which come from a number of contributors, e.g. *Society: Problems and Methods of Study* edited by A. T. Welford and others, or *Darwinism and the Study of Society* edited by Michael Banton. Whether the papers belong to one author or many, these books often deal with diverse topics and, even where a general theme runs through them, the papers cannot be regarded as representing a unified and integrated research effort. There are studies based on secondary material, however, which represent more unified attempts. Some deal for instance with sociology generally as a scientific discipline. T. B. Bottomore's *Sociology: A Guide to Problems and Literature*, and John Rex's *Key Problems of Sociological Theory* are good examples (full references have already been given). Other studies deal with specific topics. Thus taking examples from just one area, J. A. G. Griffith and others review the situation concerning race relations in Britain largely from existing material,[1] and J. A. Jackson deals with the Irish minority in Britain, which is also based on previously published material in one form or other.[2]

There are several sources of secondary material. Many studies resort to official reports and proceedings, parish registers, newspapers and periodicals, and of course books.[3] Others use existing case records,[4] or the 'who's who' type of

[1] J. A. G. Griffith *et al.*, *Coloured Immigrants in Britain*, O.U.P., 1960.
[2] J. A. Jackson, *The Irish in Britain*, Routledge, 1963.
[3] See, for instance, W. C. Dowling, 'The Ladies' Sanitary Association and the Origins of the Health Visiting Service', unpbl. M.A. thesis, Univ. of London, 1963.
[4] See R. A. Parker, 'The Application of Predictive Techniques to the

material.[1] Biographies can provide both quantitative and qualitative material and are an important source for sociological research. The kind of special problem encountered by researchers relying on secondary material can be illustrated through the following two studies. J. A. and Olive Banks in their work on *Feminism and Family Planning in Victorian England* draw our attention to the fact that their reading of the relevant published material was bound to be interpretive. In order to escape the charge of obscurantism they provide, therefore, 'a full documentary of [their] sources of information so that those who desire to challenge results may freely use the material accessible to [them]. In no other way does it seem at present that the systematic and disciplined approach of sociology can be applied to the study of *social change* where the data has been recorded, but not for sociological purposes, in the past.'[2] In a complex statistical study of social and economic differences of *British Towns*, Moser and Scott demonstrate the kind of selectivity necessary where, although most of the sources provide straightforward statistical data which are unlikely to contain any subjectivity, some of the sources may be found unsuitable for the particular study. Thus it was the 1951 census of population for England and

---

Practice of Social Work', unpbl. PH.D. thesis, Univ. of London, 1961; and his *Decision in Child Care: a Study of Prediction in Fostering*, Allen & Unwin, 1966; and N. Timms, 'Techniques, Theory and Viewpoint in English Social Casework', unpbl. M.A. thesis, Univ. of London, 1960. Sometimes case histories are built up by means of a series of interviews specifically carried out for the research in hand; otherwise case histories are obtained from existing records. For the former technique see Patricia Ball, 'A Study of Extra-Marital Pregnancy', unpbl. M.A. thesis, Univ. of Liverpool, 1962, p. 50ff; for the latter technique see Sarah F. McCabe, 'A Study of the Treatment of Delinquent Girls', unpbl. B.Litt. thesis, Univ. of Oxford, 1964, p. 43ff.

[1] See T. J. H. Bishop, *Winchester and the Public School Elite*, Faber, 1967.

[2] *op. cit.*, p. 135.

Wales that provided the main source. Certain relevant statistics of the wide range published by the Registrar-General for England and Wales were also used. And as Moser and Scott say, 'Various other sources have been utilized'. Thus, 'The Board of Trade Census of Distribution 1950 yielded the data on retail sales; statistics of new housing have been taken from the quarterly returns of the Ministry of Housing and Local Government; election statistics from *The Times Guide to the House of Commons for 1951 and 1955*; the J-index from a Government social survey publication, and so forth'.[1] On the other hand the financial and administrative statistics of local authorities were not used, as this required specialist knowledge and a more detailed treatment than the authors had time to give. The results of relevant sample surveys were also not utilized since these covered only a few of the 157 towns included in the study.

Against the studies which rely entirely on secondary material must be set those which use partly or exclusively primary data. The latter may be obtained either through the survey technique or by means of participant observation. The survey technique, relying on systematic random sampling and carried out either through personal interviews or postal questionnaires, appears to be much favoured in British sociological research. A few of the many examples that could be given will be selected here to highlight points of special interest. The electoral register has been used as a sampling frame in many studies,[2] but numerous other frames can be encountered, e.g. records of doctors' practices, membership lists of institutions, 'addressograph files', or records of

---

[1] *op. cit.*, pp. 7, 8.
[2] See P. Willmott and M. Young, *Family and Class in a London Suburb*, Routledge, 1960, pp. x, 133; P. Collison, *The Cutteslowe Walls*, Faber, 1963, pp. 174–6; C. Vereker and J. B. Mays, *Urban Redevelopment and Social Change*, Liverpool U.P., 1961, p. 123.

students in academic institutions.[1] It must be noted, however, that although some studies claim to have obtained 'sample data', the representativeness of the latter is in question due to the lack of a sampling frame and selection from it in accordance with statistical requirements. F. Zweig, for instance, relates how 'hourly-rated men with a *sprinkling* [our italics] of weekly paid supervisors were chosen at random'[2] in a study of factory workers, but gives no details of the system he used and leaves the impression that no particular attention was paid to survey-technique principles.

In other studies, however, it is freely admitted that valid samples were unobtainable. A case in point is Sheila Patterson's study of West Indians in south London where a representative sample was impossible to obtain 'by reason of the recent arrival of most members, of the changing demographic structure of the groups and of its high mobility'.[3] She sought, therefore, the point of contact in the various major areas of association, and her study can be regarded as being based on a 'survey' only in the broader sense of that word. An interesting example of work where resources were too limited to allow the drawing of a random sample, shows that nevertheless an attempt was made to adopt some kind of selection procedure into which subjectivity was unlikely to enter. Thus in Pearl Jephcott's study of conditions in multi-occupied houses in Notting Hill the following steps were taken: 'A circle was drawn with a radius of 1,500 feet from the local tube station on a 1:2500 map of Kensington; this circle contained a certain number of streets, from each of which house numbers x, $x + 1$

---

[1] See Willmott and Young, *ibid.*; B. A. McFarlane, 'The Chartered Engineer', unpbl. PH.D. thesis, Univ. of London, 1961, p. 15; G. L. Millerson, *The Qualifying Associations*, Routledge, 1964; L. F. Douglas, 'Types of Students and their Outlook on University Education', unpbl. PH.D. thesis, Univ. of London, 1964.

[2] *The Worker in an Affluent Society*, Heinemann, 1961, p. xiii.

[3] *op. cit.*, p. 26.

and $x-1$ were selected.'[1] There are, however, cases where the use of any kind of sampling frame, whether maps, lists or other existing records, is simply not feasible, due to the fact that the population which one attempts to sample is not known. G. Westwood in his study of homosexuals makes this point. He nevertheless claimed that he was able to achieve a fairly representative sample by the 'grapevine' method. He built up a chain-reaction whereby the friends of those interviewed (and the friends of their friends) agreed to cooperate. As he points out this procedure must be limited (in his case he accepted three contacts from one source), for otherwise the whole sample could come from the same closed circle.[2]

Some studies make use of the 'follow-up survey', which is of particular advantage where the researcher is primarily concerned with an occurrence or with the effects of a new phenomenon bringing about basic changes. Thus Ruth Glass and J. Westergaard, in considering the development of the new community of Lansbury, started off with a survey in which they attempted to interview all the 168 newly settled householders on the estate. A year later follow-up enquiries were started, which were taken up again six years later. It is interesting to note that according to Ruth Glass the study of Lansbury was itself 'part of a continuing series of enquiries, carried out or initiated by the Centre for Urban Studies through which the changing structure of metropolitan society and culture will be explored'.[3] Here is, then, an example of a 'follow-up' survey used within the general pattern or framework of a number of linked enquiries over a period of time.

[1] P. Jephcott, *A Troubled Area*, Faber, 1964, pp. 35–41.

[2] Westwood, *op. cit.*, p. 197.

[3] Ruth Glass *et al.*, *London—Aspects of Change*, McGibbon & Kee, 1964, pp. 160–1, xxxvi. Some of the points regarding general frameworks, continuity, etc., will be discussed in greater detail below, see pp. 187f, 207f.

Probably the best example of a longitudinal survey is that which originated in the national sample of mothers who provided information in 1946 about the provisions and uses made of antenatal and maternity services. The initial sample of nearly 13,000 children, who had been born to these mothers in one week in March 1946, was cut down to half when the decision was taken to carry out a number of follow-up studies. These were undertaken at fairly short intervals under the direction of J. W. B. Douglas; the topics investigated ranging from types of illness among the children when under five, to experiences in primary education, secondary education, and so on.[1]

Considering a more limited use of the longitudinal survey we find a sample survey in which G. E. Levens used four separate interviews in connection with the study of the occupational and social mobility of 'white-collar criminals'. The first interview took place in prison during the last few weeks of serving their sentence and was used as a preparatory interview to establish rapport with the offenders. Then at approximately one month, four months and eight months after discharge, respondents were interviewed again, in order to trace the effects of imprisonment upon occupational and social position.[2]

Surveys are often divided into several stages, each one of which serves different purposes. In a study of Indian students in Britain A. K. Singh used the first stage for distributing an extensive questionnaire with mainly 'closed' questions to the full sample, in addition to which he used a supplementary

[1] J. W. B. Douglas and J. M. Blomfield, *Children Under Five*, Allen & Unwin, 1958; and J. W. B. Douglas, *The Home and the School*, MacGibbon & Kee, 1964. This particular longitudinal survey will be discussed again below, see p. 195.

[2] G. E. Levens, 'A Study of the Occupational and Social Mobility of "White-collar Criminals" after their Discharge from Prison', unpbl. M.SC. thesis, Univ. of London, 1964.

questionnaire, with a sub-sample, in order to gain more detailed and qualitative information mainly through 'open-ended' questions.[1] Willmott and Young's study of a London suburb used a large general sample covering all adults in Woodford, a smaller old-age sample drawn from those of pensionable age, and the marriage sample which was an even smaller special group, being a sub-sample of the general sample and containing parents with at least two children under 15 who were subjected to more intensive interviewing.[2] It is obvious that in many studies such as this, general information must be supplemented with more detailed and specialized material concerning certain groups.

One way of supplementing and filling out basic information gathered in a survey is to arrange with a sub-sample to keep a diary of daily activities over a period of time. This technique was used by Peter Willmott in his study of *Adolescent Boys in East London*, who sets out clearly the kind of instructions that may be given to diarists.[3]

In some studies the intensive interview, often applied to smaller non-randomly selected groups, is the main research technique. Sheila Patterson resorted, for example, to long, often repeated and completely informal, but intensive interviews. She even argued that in interviewing relatively unsophisticated people the production of paper and pencil by the interviewer would have had an inhibiting effect on the interviewee.[4] But the advantages of such informality may be outweighed by the resultant 'memory errors', due to there being no recording of the interview on the spot. Another point of criticism must be made here. This is the possibility of a bias produced, regarding the information gleaned from the

[1] A. K. Singh, *Indian Students in Britain*, Asia Publishing House, 1963.
[2] *op. cit.*, pp. x, 133.
[3] Routledge, 1966, appendix 3.
[4] *op. cit.*, p. 27.

coloured minority, as a result of the interviewer not belonging to the West Indian group. For 'there is an abundance of experimental evidence to prove that bias may result, under certain conditions, regardless of anything the interviewer may do to eliminate it', due to the interviewer not belonging to the group studied.[1] Patterson argues, however, that the white investigator is probably in a better position for undertaking studies of race relations in Britain than a coloured investigator would be.[2] There is of course a way out; the investigation could ideally be carried out by a team composed of individuals fully acceptable in the various groups under scrutiny. Barring this, it is probably true that any bias that may enter at the data-gathering stage can best be reduced through the informal intensive interviews to which Patterson resorted.

In another study we find again the intensive interview used, albeit in a more structured manner. But at the same time care was taken to make sure that the interviewer was acceptable as a member of the in-group investigated. As Joan Brothers tells us, in her study of the impact of education on the Catholic Church in Liverpool, 'information would not have been disclosed frankly . . . to non-Catholics'.[3] In contrast to Brothers' more structured interviews one can mention F. Zweig's use of the 'friendly and informal chat' in some of the workers' homes who had been previously interviewed at the factory.[4] It appears, therefore, that the interview as a technique varies in these studies from intensive, and sometimes structured, confrontations to informal meetings or even light chats. Similarly the questionnaire or schedule was at times a fairly rigid tool mainly to obtain basic and wide-ranging

---

[1] C. Selltiz *et al.*, *Research Methods in Social Relations*, Henry Holt, New York, 1959, p. 584.
[2] *op. cit.*, p. 32ff.
[3] *op. cit.*, p. 32.
[4] *op. cit.*, p. xi.

information and at other times a more flexible technique intent on gaining a deeper understanding of a situation.

The factors that must inevitably govern the choice of techniques are (a) their suitability in given circumstances; (b) the kind of results desired; and (c) the likely reliability of the results.

We shall now return to a consideration of the population investigated and the samples upon which the investigations have been based. From the discussion, so far, of the sample survey technique it may have been erroneously assumed that such sampling techniques apply only to studies involving the first-hand collection of data. This is certainly not the case. The principles of sampling can be applied to situations where data is extracted from existing recorded information. To give just one example, Ruth Glass in her study of West Indian immigrants in London used the records kept about the immigrants at the offices of the Migrant Services Division of the West Indian Commission. Of the 5,000 cards with data, relevant information was extracted for 1,070 individuals and this was termed as the 'London Sample'. It is true that the original population represented by the 5,000 cards consisted of a voluntary body of migrants who chose to consult the Division's offices, a fact which might have suggested the possibility of unrepresentativeness. Ruth Glass says, however, that certain available external data made possible a detailed comparison with the sample results, which 'led to the conclusion that the London Sample can be regarded with confidence, in particular so far as male migrants are concerned'.[1] The problem of drawing samples from special groups or institutions has also been faced, for instance in medicine, where hospital samples are frequently unrepresentative. The Medical Research Council has sponsored intensive studies of particular communities, for example in the Rhondda Valley,

[1] Ruth Glass, *Newcomers: The West Indians in London*, Centre for Urban Studies and Allen & Unwin, 1960, pp. 11, 12.

and also members of the Royal College of General Practitioners have organized case-finding investigations covering groups of general practices which could be taken to be sufficiently representative of the general population.[1]

The sampling technique can be employed, therefore, either for gaining first-hand information through postal questionnaires and interviewing or for extracting information from existing records. Whatever the case, the population covered will depend on such factors as the topic dealt with, the resources available to the researcher, and the techniques most suitable for the enquiry in question. We find broadly two categories: (a) where a contiguous area or population is covered, e.g. which is particularly the case where community structures or group relations are investigated; (b) where a special population is looked for which is spread over a larger area, e.g. schoolchildren or professional people, and where the sample may come from (one or several) specialized units containing such populations. Good examples are for (a) the studies by Willmott and Young and by Patterson where Woodford and Brixton, two districts in London, were covered respectively,[2] and for (b) the studies by Brothers, who has drawn her sample from nine Catholic grammar schools, and by Millerson, whose sample came from the members of three professional associations.[3]

As far as sample size is concerned, this varies from the relatively large sample designed to produce basic factual information, often to serve as background of studies, to the much smaller sample selected for eliciting more detailed and often qualitative information which would allow the investigator to delve deeply into special problems. The same study may contain several samples serving such different purposes.

---

[1] I am grateful to Dr H. Merskey for providing me with this information.
[2] Willmott and Young, *op. cit.*, pp. x, 133; Patterson, *op. cit.*, p. 27.
[3] Brothers, *op. cit.*, p. 22; Millerson, *op. cit.*

Thus, Willmott and Young used a large sample of 939 individuals to cover the whole community of Woodford and and two smaller samples of 210 and 44 respondents to provide material respectively on old people and on married people with younger children in the district. Similarly F. Zweig interviewed 672 workers in several factories (plus some 200 managers and foremen), and also visited 60 homes of workers already interviewed in the factories. The latter provided him with a sub-sample of the main sample.[1] Another relatively large sample was that used by Vereker and Mays to cover the Crown Street district of Liverpool. It totalled 574 households and it comprised one in 20 of all the households in the district.[2] Some much smaller samples, serving nonetheless as backbones of the enquiries, have also been used. Thus, P. Collison's sample comprised 203 respondents but an attempt was made to re-interview them; in 155 cases this was successful, so that in fact more than 350 interviews were carried out.[3] S. Patterson interviewed some 250 white people and about 150 coloured immigrants. Once again the actual samples are small but the total interviews come to about 400.[4] These may also have been much more time-consuming owing to the intensive nature of the interviews. Finally we come across the much smaller samples either due to the nature of the population on which it is difficult to draw for respondents, or because the enquiry is regarded as no more than a pilot investigation. Thus, examples for the former would be the 94 men sampled from six prisons to study the social and occupational mobility of 'white-collar criminals'[5] or the 127 individuals interviewed on the subject of homosexuality.[6] Examples for the latter

---

[1] Zweig, *op. cit.*, pp. x–xiii.
[2] Vereker and Mays, *op. cit.*, pp. 8, 124.
[3] Collison, *op. cit.*, pp. 174–6 and appendix A.
[4] Patterson, *op. cit.*, p. 27.
[5] G. E. Levens, *op. cit.*
[6] G. Westwood, *op. cit.*, p. 197.

would be the 84 interviews completed by Brothers regarding the impact of grammar-school education on religious attitudes[1] or the 40 families studied by Baskerville in Greenwich.[2] It should be noted that, whilst the proportion of the sample to the whole population is immaterial as far as statistical treatment of the results is concerned, the actual size of the sample is most important from the point of view of the analysis, in that if numerous breakdowns are wanted in the tabulations the sub-groups or cells would contain too few units for the results to remain meaningful.[3] But where a small sample is used for intensive interviewing and the results are not presented in quantitative form, such problem of sample size does not arise. Many an example, such as the study by Brothers or Patterson, could be quoted to show this, but we shall return to this discussion when dealing with the analysis of field material in the next section.

It is of some interest to note two points related in particular to surveys conducted through postal questionnaires. First, that the original samples encountered have not been very different, as far as size is concerned, from samples used in surveys relying on interviews. Secondly, that the non-response rate was generally high. Thus, A. K. Singh started out with a sample of 710 but collected only 69 per cent of completed questionnaires.[4] From B. A. MacFarlane's sample of 500 only 44 per cent of replies were used in the analysis.[5] In a postal survey conducted by F. Musgrove the final sample consisted of 200 respondents and this reflected a response of only 30 per cent.[6] Similarly in G. L. Millerson's postal

---

[1] J. Brothers, *op. cit.*, p. 22.

[2] D. R. Baskerville, *op. cit.*

[3] See C. A. Moser, *Survey Methods in Social Investigation*, Heinemann, 1958, p. 117.

[4] *op. cit.*

[5] *op. cit.*, p. 19.

[6] *Youth and the Social Order*, Routledge, 1964, pp. 11, 12.

enquiry the response was disappointing.[1] In comparison, the Willmott and Young study's main survey was afflicted by a non-response of only 10 per cent.[2] This percentage represents, however, only refusals. But even if we add the 'non-contacts' to produce a figure which is more fairly comparable with 'non-response' in postal enquiries, this was still only 20 per cent. In P. Collison's first survey non-response amounted to 15.4 per cent and even re-interviewing was successfully carried out with 76 per cent of the original respondents.[3] Non-response is a serious problem in that, if it occurs even to a moderate degree, it could vitiate the findings.

Another major sociological research tool, besides the survey technique, is that of observation. It is natural for the latter to prove more advantageous in certain circumstances, particularly where, due to the subject matter, for instance, such indirect ways are likely to yield less biased results than formal interviews might do. Observation may be concealed, as used mainly by psychologists in laboratory conditions; it may be disguised or undisguised, either of the participating or non-participating variety, as used mainly by sociologists and anthropologists.[4] Although what is essentially non-participant observation is quite frequently employed, as for instance in some of the researches of the Institute of Community Studies, in very many studies a certain degree of participation seems to be favoured where observation techniques are used. One example of full participation is given by Tom Lupton's long stretch of actual work in factories where he chose to use 'open participant observation'.[5] A high degree of participation

[1] *op. cit.*

[2] *op. cit.*, p. 136.

[3] *op. cit.*, pp. 174–6 and appendix A.

[4] For a clear distinction of different types of observation see: Michael Argyle, *The Scientific Study of Social Behaviour*, Methuen, 1957, pp. 34–6.

[5] T. Lupton, *On the Shop Floor*, Pergamon, 1963, p. vii and appendix 1,

seems also to have been achieved by R. Frankenberg, who lived for 12 months in the North-Wales village which he studied.[1] In some of the studies we quote below, participation appears often to have been rather more interrupted and not quite so fully utilized.[2]

The great value of the technique of observation is proved by its use in many of the sociological studies in combination with the survey technique. Thus, Willmott and Young say: 'We have depended mainly but not entirely on the interviews. We also tried to keep our eyes open during the three years we spent on the enquiry and observed as much of interest as we could about Woodford people in public places like streets, shops and trains'.[3] Margaret Stacey in her study of Banbury also used a combination of techniques. She points out that participant observation is inadequate for a town the size of Banbury and that, therefore, she combined it with the use of published records and the survey technique. But she states that throughout the research the members of the team made their homes in or near Banbury and thus 'participation in the life of the town was a main method of the work'. It is also interesting to note that there was a division of labour within the team, each one participating in a different sphere of the town's life.[4] Sheila Patterson, too, has used a combination of techniques. She describes how she spent four to five days, and often evenings, in the Brixton neighbourhood 'interviewing, observing or participating in various local or immigrant

---

p. 202. The best example of disguised participant observation is the American study by Leon Festinger *et al.*, *When Prophecy Fails*, Univ. of Minnesota Press, Minneapolis, 1956, esp. p. 237.

   [1] R. Frankenberg, *Village on the Border*, Cohen & West, 1957, pp. vii, viii, 148.

   [2] I am much indebted to J. A. Banks for valuable suggestions in connection with the technique of observation.

   [3] *op. cit.*, p. x.

   [4] Stacey, *op. cit.*, p. v.

activities'.[1] The present writer in his study of Jews in Leeds also combined participant observation with other techniques. As pointed out in that connection the problem with participant observation is that of achieving sufficient familiarity and acceptance for the participation of the researcher not to be regarded as 'different' from participation by others, and at the same time for the former to be able to maintain an objective outlook. Thus the writer has claimed that in his study he was fortunate to achieve just such a balance: 'I lived in Leeds for seven years prior to embarking on the field research. I was, thus, not a stranger but thoroughly acquainted with the community, and participated in its life. I happened to know many of the communal leaders, and had easy entrée to most of them. The ordinary folk regarded me as one of themselves. My knowledge of Yiddish and Hebrew, and of the *haim* (literally 'home'—Eastern Europe) where I was brought up, were most valuable assets. At the same time I was familiar with the general Anglo-Jewish scene, with which I first made contact in the East End and then in North London. In spite of my relatively long stay in Leeds and my participation in the life of the community, I still regarded myself as somewhat of an outsider and could look upon the community in such a capacity, and so attempt to maintain a valuable objectivity'.[2] Many other examples can be given where participant observation was employed at least as one of several techniques.[3]

But participant observation, as the main technique, really comes into its own in the setting of smaller and more isolated but intimate groups. Thus, it was used in this way to very great advantage by James Littlejohn in his study of *Westrigg*, a Cheviot parish. Littlejohn was interested in particular in the

[1] Patterson, *op. cit.*, p. 27.
[2] Krausz, *op. cit.*, p. vii.
[3] To give just two further examples one may mention W. M. Williams, *A West Country Village: Ashworthy*, Routledge, 1963; and Elspeth Huxley, *Back Street New Worlds*, Chatto, 1964.

stratification system prevalent in that community. He used participant observation in the following ways: (a) 'listening in conversation with and among parishioners for words implying a conventional classification of persons and families falling within the various classes'; (b) 'noting friendships and cliques among parishioners and placing them within these classes'; and (c) 'noting association and interaction among them on public occasions'.[1]

Particular problems were encountered in the study of a prison where observation was used as the main technique for gathering data. The study is that of *Pentonville* in London carried out by Terence and Pauline Morris.[2] According to the authors the technique employed consisted in essence 'in *being on the premises*, visibly yet unobtrusively, and engaging in informal conversation whenever the opportunity presented itself'.[3] There were several problems encountered. Despite the acute physical isolation of the group studied, the latter's composition was relatively unstable—of a prison population of some 1,200 men, about 15 were received and 15 were discharged each day. A 'Hawthorne effect' was created, in that members of the prison community were conscious of the research, and their behaviour was sometimes 'adjusted' with this in mind both consciously and unconsciously. It was difficult to gain cooperation with both prisoners and staff and at the same time avoid identification with either of the groups. A major problem was also the communication of the objects of the research and the clearing of misleading notions about the researchers being in the employment of the Home Office. A tremendous problem was created initially by the fact that

[1] Routledge, 1963, p. 76.

[2] *op. cit.* Some fieldwork was carried out in Maidstone during July and Aug. 1958, but the main part of the enquiry consisted of the fieldwork carried out in Pentonville continuously from Oct. 1958 to Jan. 1960 (see p. 7).

[3] *ibid.*, p. 8.

the principal research worker was a woman.[1] Except for the last problem mentioned, the difficulties enumerated appear to have been in the main unavoidable, and despite these problems observation seemed a flexible enough instrument to be used in research concerned with the special type of human group that a prison community represents.

Participant observation has been modified and given a special slant in the instrument for fact-gathering produced by Tom Harrison and his colleagues, which was labelled 'mass observation'. According to Harrison 'mass observation' is a two-pronged technique whereby the *mass* is observed through 'the field study of actual behaviour under normal living conditions', and the mass observes itself through 'self documentation and "subjective" reportage, including the network of voluntary, candid informants in all walks of life'.[2] More concisely the technique reflects primarily a concerted effort by a group to observe life around them, in this case the central piece of observation having been 'Worktown', an industrial town in the north. Charles Madge, himself a member of the original team of 'mass observation' has recognized the drawbacks of what has been called the 'natural history' approach. These have been the lack of clear objectives and orientations insofar as the field work was concerned and the resultant indiscriminate interest which was reflected in the hotch-potch character of the results. He argues, nevertheless, that the mixed bag of observation produced 'some sort of a net [which] had been spread to catch that fleeting, glinting apparition, the essence of time'.[3] This could prove, therefore, an important and flexible instrument to record the changing patterns of society over time.

Another unconventional approach used in several studies is

[1] *ibid.*, pp. 6–11.
[2] Tom Harrison, *Britain Revisited*, Gollancz, 1961, p. 17.
[3] See postscript by Charles Madge, *ibid.*, pp. 277, 278, 280.

what bears such names as 'action research', 'operational research' or 'sociotherapeutic research'. A detailed account of the principles and aims of such research is given by John Spencer and his collaborators. They were concerned with the study of the 'stresses and strains' of a developing community in Bristol, and the main aspects of their work, as given below, describe the fundamental nature of action research: (1) close collaboration between the layman and the professional team; (2) the use of a problem-centred approach; and (3) the intention of helping to bring about change in an existing situation.[1] It should be noted that within the context of action research, conventional techniques are used, as for instance in the case quoted above surveys and participant observation were used.[2] The distinguishing feature of action research is, therefore, not in the details of technique. It is to be found basically, as Spencer says, in that whilst the conventional social scientist isolates the problem under investigation and relies on the systematic testing of hypotheses, such a process is not possible in action research. It is true that the starting point in action research, too, is some problem; in the above study it was juvenile delinquency. But the problem is 'constantly reformulated through subsequent reflection and experience'.[3] The inability to test hypotheses has been severely criticized, and Spencer recognizes that action research does not aim at establishing laws about human nature and cannot be regarded as pure research.[4] But the advantage claimed for this kind of procedure is its ability to facilitate change. Thus, in addition to the complex nature of the field of social research, even greater fluidity is introduced into the situation.

[1] John Spencer *et al.*, *Stress and Release in an Urban Estate: a Study in Action Research*, Tavistock, 1964, p. 20.

[2] *ibid.*, pp. 10, 16.

[3] *ibid.*, p. 24.

[4] *ibid.*, p. 20.

But then this is to be expected where innovation through social action is the main aim. An interesting example of action research is provided by the second project carried out by Pearl Jephcott in connection with her study of multi-occupied housing in Notting Hill. After the study of the main problems she attempted to induce local residents to cooperate in short-term and small-scale action regarding such problems as the provision of outdoor play facilities for small children.[1] Another instance of action research, or as Mays calls it 'operational research', was the boys' club experiment which he utilized in order to discover the effectiveness of group-work in promoting the adjustment of delinquent and near-delinquent boys. Further he wanted to see how this technique could be combined with other therapeutic techniques and to find out what influence the contact of leaders with parents could have on the boys. There was also an interest to learn how far other social workers and agencies were willing to collaborate.[2]

It must be noted that action research often relies on a multi-discipline approach. In the Bristol project sociology and psychiatry have played important roles.[3] In this connection we may consider also other researchers influenced by psychiatry. There is for instance the social-analytic approach developed by Elliot Jaques. Unlike 'action research' social analysis 'does not urge a particular course of action' and the analyst 'is not personally embroiled in the organization and its problems'.[4] What happens is that when help is sought from an analyst regarding a problem faced by an organization, his task is to determine the nature of the problem. He is to do

[1] Jephcott, *op. cit.*
[2] J. B. Mays, *On the Threshold of Delinquency*, Liverpool U.P., 1959, pp. 22, 192.
[3] Spencer, *op. cit.*, pp. 61ff.
[4] E. Jaques, 'Social Analysis and the Glacier Project', in W. Brown and E. Jaques, *Glacier Project Papers*, Heinemann, 1965, p. 34.

this from an independent position. Jaques adopted his approach from the field of psycho-analysis to study a multitude of problems of social organization, industrial relations and management in connection with the Glacier project.[1] A similar model of social consultancy, but with a socio-therapeutic concern, was used by Cyril Sofer in a study of organizational behaviour. His approach was 'influenced by psychological thinking of the psychoanalytic variety and by the structural school of British social anthropology'.[2] The organizations studied comparatively included an industrial concern, a medical research unit and an educational establishment. All these different kinds of approach, and action research generally, have special leanings and emphases, but at the same time they usually contain many of the techniques normally used for data collection in sociological research.

Analysis and interpretation

The analysis and interpretation of the material collected, whether from secondary sources or from fieldwork, are the most difficult tasks and require the greatest skill of the researcher. Although some of the studies considered have been given more to description than to explanation, most contain analysis of the kind that attempts to relate variables and thus to provide explanations for the existence of certain social phenomena. We shall not discuss here whether the causal explanation is possible in sociology or, for that matter, in any discipline,[3] although many a conclusion based on the analysis of sociological research material purports to do just that. We must be content with furnishing some idea of the way such analysis has been carried out in sociological research.

[1] *ibid.*, p. 30.

[2] Cyril Sofer, *The Organization From Within*, Tavistock, 1961, p. xiii. Sociotherapeutic and action research studies of the type discussed in this study have been conducted by the Tavistock Institute of Human Relations (*ibid.*, p. xi).

[3] See ch. 1, above.

It is evident that some studies fall in the category in which the analysis of the material, i.e. the sifting of information, the numerous attempts to relate variables, the presentation of results etc., has hardly been aided by any standardized techniques. The techniques are rather individualistic and flexible. This applies equally to studies with a theoretical or historical perspective and to those based on field research and dealing with the contemporary scene. Thus studies such as those of J. A. and Olive Banks on family planning in Victorian England, of David Martin on the ideology of pacifism, of J. A. Jackson regarding the Irish in Britain, of J. Nagel regarding the writings of Karl Marx, or of S. Andreski dealing with such topics as feudalism, have not relied on any recognizable standard techniques in their analysis. Neither has such reliance been much in evidence in some of the studies based on field work, such as Sheila Patterson's work on West Indian immigrants or F. Zweig's study of factory workers. Joan Brothers, another sociologist who has not used standardized techniques for analysis, explains that this was due to the fact that in her study of the impact of education on religion, some of the most fruitful information, and most of the results in fact, defied statistical treatment even of the simplest kind, e.g. tabulation.[1] She claims, however, that this was not a drawback, but on the contrary it led to a deeper understanding of the working of the social system investigated. It cannot be denied that there are certain advantages in the procedure, in which there is not the rigidity of the kind where information has to fit preconceived categories or where the interrelating of variables depends on some computer programme. The possibility of shifting backwards and forwards in comparing pieces of evidence, of changing midway the whole pattern of the analysis, score in favour of the non-standardized and entirely flexible type of analysis.

[1] *op. cit.*, pp. 33, 34.

The second category of studies is that in which great reliance is placed on standardized techniques[1] for the processing and analysis of the material, and these include the use of coding devices, machine tabulation, attitude scaling, significance testing, multivariate analysis, and factor analysis. Many of the studies based on surveys, and also some using data from secondary sources, resort to the well-known techniques of quantification; and they often present the figures in cross-tabulated form which provides the elementary type of statistical measurement and analysis that shows up relationships between variables. But whilst we often come across frequency tables, percentages, indices, and measures of central tendency, the more sophisticated types of measurement techniques and analytical tools are rarely met.

Thus, attitude scaling as a measuring device has been used only in a few studies. There are various scaling techniques designed to 'assess intensities of attitudes or opinions',[2] but their application in each study may require quite lengthy preparatory work. Nevertheless some studies have employed such techniques. Thus, F. Musgrove used several scaling techniques, one of which was the Social Distance Scale to measure the social gap between generations.[3] Alan Little used, for instance, the Guttman Scale to measure the Borstal inmates' attitude towards the staff and the system and so to test his hypothesis that an anti-staff and anti-system culture

[1] It may be mentioned here that the standardization of questionnaires is necessary in order to overcome the idiosyncrasy of the individual researcher and so achieve objectivity. Studies of secondary data can be carried on quite successfully without this, unless a larger content analysis programme is under way, because provided that all the sources are given, a later researcher can look at the same material to test and re-analyse the earlier study. This is not possible with field research unless standardized procedures are adopted.

[2] M. Duverger, *Introduction to the Social Sciences*, Allen & Unwin, 1964, p. 198.

[3] *op. cit.*, pp. 11, 12, 89, 90.

prevailed.[1] Another example is C. E. Fiscian's use of the Authoritarian Scale to measure minority group prejudice.[2]

Even rarer, however, than the use of attitude scales seems to be the use of the more advanced techniques for analysing complex relationships between several variables. One such technique is that of multivariate analysis, and this was used by Moser and Scott in their study of the social and economic differences of *British Towns*, a study in which the interrelationship of 57 variables was analysed.[3] A refinement was introduced by the use of component analysis. Another technique for dealing with complex phenomena is that of factor analysis and this was employed by L. F. Douglas in his comparative study of types of students and their outlook on university education, in which he used 14 statements to analyse the main factors underlying the differences between the types of students.[4] Finally, regression analysis is an important technique in that it provides the possibility of obtaining more accurate estimates and of making more reliable predictions.[5] Pauline Morris in her study of families of imprisoned men regarded adjustment to separation as a dependent variable and environmental factors, such as length of sentence, husband's occupation, wife's age, etc., as independent variables. A linear regression model was then tested for 10 such items.[6] These techniques that we have mentioned involve mathematical procedures and the acceptance of certain models which may be difficult to fit to the type of research material produced within the sociological field. The

[1] Little, *op. cit.*, p. 130.

[2] *op. cit.*

[3] *op. cit.*, p. 66ff.

[4] *op. cit.*, pp. 158, 289.

[5] See G. Milton Smith, *A Simplified Guide to Statistics* (3rd ed.), Holt, Rinehart, New York, 1962, pp. 97, 108ff.

[6] Pauline Morris, *Prisoners and their Families*, appendix D, pp. 310, 311.

techniques themselves may have to be modified to suit sociology,[1] and it should be noted that two of the examples given above could in fact be regarded as taken from the allied disciplines of demography and social psychology rather than from sociology proper.[2]

Although the more sophisticated analytical techniques are as yet rare in sociology, certain tools have been employed more often, as for instance the calculation of correlations between two variables.[3] Even more widespread, however, is the use of the test of statistical significance in sociological research.[4] This was a natural development following the increase in the number of random sample surveys carried out by sociologists. But the random sample survey has its limitation. As Festinger and Katz point out: 'Any data-gathering project based on a sample is subject to sampling error. This means that all findings coming from such a study must be interpreted in the light of this error. This limitation becomes particularly important when a total sample is divided into parts for purposes of analysis'.[5] In an effort to establish whether differences in the sample data, say a given percentage difference

---

[1] See Grebenik and Moser in Welford *et al.*, *Society*, *op. cit.*, p. 21. For a further discussion of this problem see below, pp. 199, 209.

[2] The studies have, however, sufficient sociological orientation to be included in our review.

[3] To give just one example, Ann Cartwright calculated the correlations between hospitalization rates on the one hand and proportion of people aged 65 and more, social-class indices, and changes in the size of populations in different areas, on the other (Ann Cartwright, *Human Relations and Hospital Care*, Routledge, 1964, p. 244).

[4] One can gauge to some extent how widespread the use of tests of significance has become from the fact that in a sample of the studies considered in this volume, covering the period 1960–4, of 46 pieces of research which included some fieldwork, 27 resorted to random sampling and of these 11 used tests of significance.

[5] L. Festinger and D. Katz (eds.), *Research Methods in the Behavioral Sciences*, Holt, Rinehart, New York, 1953, p. 49.

between two sub-groups in the sample, is due to sampling error or if it in fact represents a real difference in the universe, the test of significance is introduced. This simply establishes the probability that the difference in question cannot be accounted for by sampling error, and if this probability is high (usually 0.90 or 0.95) the conclusion is reached that there is a true difference. Attention has been drawn to the caution necessary when using such tests in analysis and interpretation. Thus, Moser warns against an 'excessive emphasis on significance tests, to the detriment of the estimation of the magnitude of effects'.[1] In other words, a result which is statistically significant may nevertheless, through lack of magnitude, be of little interest to the researcher and, vice versa, a result which is not statistically significant may nevertheless be of importance in a particular context. Furthermore, as Goode and Hatt say, where sample figures are given it must be constantly borne in mind that 'we cannot know how close our data are to the universe parameters',[2] for we are dealing with probabilities.

But there has been more than just warnings regarding the use of tests of significance. Among American sociologists a dispute has been raging in the last 10 years concerning the very 'legitimacy' of such tests in sociological research. Prominent among those who have called into question the validity of tests of significance in survey research data has been Hanan C. Selvin. His line of reasoning may be summarized as follows: (a) in sociological research it is hardly ever possible to achieve *experimental control*; (b) to overcome the inability to control 'all relevant factors' the technique of randomization should be employed, but this is not possible in sociological research—the random assignment of subjects

---

[1] *op. cit.*, p. 294.
[2] W. J. Goode and P. K. Hatt, *Methods in Social Research*, McGraw-Hill, New York, 1952, p. 372.

to experimental and control groups is applicable only in the rare cases of laboratory studies or policy-oriented experiments; (c) randomization would remove the systematic effect of uncontrolled variables—'it converts systematic differences between the experimental and control groups into random differences, thus allowing the statistical measurement of the possibility that the observed differences could have been produced by the randomization'; (d) this is not to be confused with the fact that there is another source of random difference, i.e. the accidental variation produced in sampling; this, however, does not eliminate 'correlated biases'. The conclusion is, therefore, that whilst tests of significance are meaningful when applied in situations such as (c), it is not valid to employ them in connection with situations such as (d) unless correlated biases have been controlled, which is impossible in most sociological research.[1] Selvin condemned, therefore, most sociological studies using such tests, for as a rule they are used in conjunction with random sampling variation rather than randomization. These charges have been taken up by Robert McGinnis who puts forward the following main arguments against Selvin: a distinction must be made between the type of hypotheses which are tested for significance; hypotheses which seek to establish cause–effect relationships do demand randomization in order to control all correlated biases, but those which aim only at description make no such demands. Hence tests of significance can validly be applied to the latter. This leads to the question of research objectives. Selvin emphasizes explanation rather than description in sociological work. But whilst explanatory work is a most desirable goal, 'descriptive' knowledge too has considerable value. McGinnis maintains that it is better to build theories on sound descriptive knowledge, and to introduce whatever controls are possible

[1] Hanan C. Selvin, 'A Critique of Tests of Significance in Survey Research', *American Sociological Review*, vol. 22, 1957, p. 519ff.

when investigating relationships between variables, than to insist, as Selvin does, on all or nothing regarding the value of statistical tests in sociology. And he concludes: 'So long as [the sociologist's] design is as carefully constructed as possible, his measurements as accurate as instruments permit, and his interpretations no broader than the data and test procedures warrant, he is performing a worthwhile service'.[1]

A little earlier it was stated that in British studies containing survey data the use of tests of significance has become fairly frequent.[2] There is at least one study, however, which although based on survey work has, in agreement with Selvin's objections, repudiated the use of such tests. Thus, although P. Willmott had used tests of significance in earlier work published under joint authorship, he declined their use in his study of Dagenham. Since tests are used to arrive at decisions regarding the validity of results, Willmott adopted the following alternative steps: 'The first was to carry out a series of further tables to try to see if apparent differences were explained by other, incidental differences, in the various groups under examination'.[3] The second was to examine on each particular issue 'any relevant information from the survey—more "impressionistic" material from the fuller interviews, as well as any statistical data available'. Such steps are certainly useful in analysing material based on surveys, but they can serve to complement rather than replace mathematical tests. The latter need not be allowed to merely lend 'a

[1] Robert McGinnis 'Randomization and Inference in Sociological Research', *American Sociological Review*, vol. 23, 1958, p. 414.

[2] The chi-square (χ^2) has been the most frequently used test. For examples of the use of tests of significance see the following studies: P. Willmott and M. Young, *Family and Class in a London Suburb*; P. Collison, *The Cutteslowe Walls*; G. Westwood, *A Minority*; Beatrice E. Pollard, *Social Casework and the State*; F. Musgrove, *Youth and the Social Order*; A. N. Little, 'Borstal: A Study of Inmates' Attitudes to the Staff and the System': all cited earlier.

[3] P. Willmott, *The Evolution of a Community*, *op. cit.*, p. 133.

bogus air of "scientific" authority to one's findings'.[1] It is interesting to note that one researcher has adopted a compromise position. Ann Cartwright accepted some of Selvin's objections to the use of tests of significance but argued that until more appropriate techniques are developed they can be usefully employed. So, whilst she 'applied [them] constantly when looking at the data . . . and [they] influenced [her] decisions about what differences to present and how much verbal "weight" 'to attach to them',[2] she made no mention of them in the text lest they gave an unwarranted impression of precision. Peter Willmott has adopted a similar position in a later study. In it he still expresses the view that the tests are somewhat shaky because they cannot throw light on 'non-random' errors,[3] and that ' "hunting" for significant differences, as distinct from testing previously stated hypotheses, is bound to give some apparently "significant" results that have arisen by chance'. But he now also finds an advantage in having through the tests 'some objective criterion to measure "probability" '. And as he says: 'The statistical tests do, after all, take into account two crucial factors—the numbers involved and the size of the differences—and do give some indication of whether a particular difference is so small or is based on such small numbers that it might well have arisen by chance alone'. With reservations, therefore, Willmott readopted the use of tests in analysing research material but was still reluctant to reproduce them in his research report for fear of giving the misleading impression of precision.

It is difficult to accept the positions taken up in this respect by Cartwright and Willmott. For although a pragmatic

---

[1] *ibid.*

[2] Ann Cartwright, *Human Relations and Hospital Care*, appendix 5, p. 248.

[3] Peter Willmott, *Adolescent Boys of East London*, Routledge, 1966, p. 184. It may be noted here that 'non-random' errors may occur for instance in interviewing or coding.

attitude in the face of over-rigorous criticism is a reasonable line to take, the hiding of the techniques used is a more dangerous tactic than the parading of what may be misleading sophistication. There is no doubt that, properly used, tests of significance can often help the researcher to make the correct interpretations and so enhance the value of his results. It is true that the use of tests is no absolute insurance against wrong interpretations; but neither are non-mathematical or non-standardized techniques of analysis a protection against such mistakes. We need all the available techniques to detect spurious relationships.

GENERAL COMMENTS

The illustrations given in connection with the different methods and techniques used have suggested that these had often to be adjusted to the particular research situation at hand, and that they depended also on the aims of the researcher, i.e. whether a pilot study, limited local enquiry or a large-scale nation-wide investigation was being undertaken. Therefore, the diversity which we found is natural enough when the general approaches and special tools employed are viewed in this light. It should be obvious, for instance, that in certain circumstances observational techniques will yield the most reliable results, whilst in others, e.g. when trying to assess the presence or absence of attributes by age-groups, the survey technique is indispensable if some degree of accuracy is desired. It is another matter, however, when purportedly the survey technique is used but the requisite care is not taken in its application. In order to stress this point we shall contrast two studies which, although different in scale and subject matter, have employed the survey technique. Thus, in a study of social mobility, directed by David Glass, a national sample of 10,000 adult civilians aged 18 years and over was obtained by means of a two-stage stratified random-sample design. The problems of substitution were weighed up and non-response rates presented so as to enable the assessment of the sample's representativeness. Sophisticated statistical calculations were used for the presentation of results, and differences between sub-groups were assessed in this way.[1] At the other extreme we find Ferdynand Zweig's study of interests and opinions among students. In this study a claim is made, in rather vague terms, that the sample of 205 students 'give a representative cross-section of the student population'. The uncertain nature of the sample is further evidenced by the fact that only third-year students, finalists and post-graduates were selected from the *Oxford University Calendar*, but that a few first- or second-year students who came up for interviews were also included in the sample. The study started as a pilot enquiry at the outset but it soon *became* a full-scale investigation! It was agreed at the outset that two universities would be covered: one Oxbridge and the other Redbrick. Zweig then says that Oxford and Manchester were obvious choices. We may ask why? The conclusions were couched in terms of broad generalizations and some of the results appear to be meaningless.[2] It is perhaps not surprising that Zweig's study has been labelled as 'popular sociology'.[3]

Apart from the different standards of rigour applied when using the survey technique, there is also the question of the

[1] D. V. Glass (ed.), *Social Mobility in Britain*, Routledge, 1954, esp. ch. 4.

[2] Zweig, *The Student in the Age of Anxiety*, Heinemann, 1963, pp. xi, xii, 1. To quote some of the results given in numerical terms this is what Zweig states in one place: 'Out of 23 students in my sample (Oxford) coming from the working-class or lower middle-class 11 were reading science; and out of 9 working-class students 5 were reading science' (p. 4). It is difficult to see what such figures can prove.

[3] See Halloran, 'Sociology and Sociologists', in J. D. Halloran and J. Brothers (eds.), *Uses of Sociology*, Sheed & Ward, 1966, pp. 13, 14 n.3.

view taken by the researcher regarding its value. W. G. Runciman, for example, employed this technique in his study of attitudes to social inequality. Although he recognized the value of the technique in providing non-conjectural information—in his case regarding how a class of people felt about the social structure in which they lived—the survey, he maintains, is a mere extension of historical interpretation. It is a continuation of the historical discussion, outside which context it has no meaning. He also finds several weaknesses in the survey: (a) it is a poor imitation of controlled experiments; (b) although its results are reliable, these do not provide definitive explanation or proof, and raise as many questions as they answer. Finally, according to Runciman 'a survey is no more than a snap-shot of the social landscape at one place and time. It may like an aerial photograph enable us for the first time to see clearly the outline of the woods and fields: but this only increases our curiosity to look under the trees'. And then he goes on to say that his survey does not test any hypotheses, and that even if consistent correlations were produced the survey would still not provide an historical explanation.[1]

Now it seems that Runciman simply confuses method or approach with technique.[2] Thus a study which spans a long period of time will naturally use the historical approach although it may utilize survey data if such exist. This is not the same as saying that the survey *technique* is used, for in fact in the hypothetical example given the technique is that of examining available secondary information; the survey technique when used in the field furnishes primary data. In Runciman's study, in fact, the technique of gathering secondary material was used in part, and this was combined with the

[1] W. G. Runciman, *Relative Deprivation and Social Justice*, Routledge, 1966, pp. 3–8.
[2] For a brief discussion of the distinction between method and technique, see above, p. 5f.

survey technique;[1] the method or approach as a whole was historical. Runciman again shows lack of clarity in regarding the survey as a weak imitation of the controlled experiment. For it should be obvious that one may combine the latter with any one of a number of distinct techniques such as the statistical survey, participant observation, case-record gathering, and so on. Due to this basic misunderstanding Runciman is led at one and the same time to expect things from the survey which are unwarranted, and also to understate its value. Of course the survey in itself does not provide *experimental* evidence or historical explanation, but experimental designs may lead up to such evidence through the use of the survey technique, and the survey data may help one to arrive at or test historical explanations, as at one point he concedes.[2] As some of the material in the following chapter will show, survey data can provide not only general impressions, as Runciman maintains, but often detailed results through which hypotheses can be tested.

Another example can be given of a sociologist who in a different sense has misunderstood the nature of the survey technique. Geoffrey Hawthorn propagates the adoption for fertility studies of a model which can be briefly described as the self-regulatory nature of populations through tendencies towards equilibrium.[3] He then counterpoises this model to the survey, the use of which in his view is responsible for the slow progress in this field. But it is totally erroneous to impute to the survey any of the true properties of a model, which is an impression one gains from Hawthorn's contrasting of his own model with the survey.[4] It is even erroneous to claim, as Hawthorn does, that the survey is wedded to the

---

[1] *ibid.*, compare Parts 2 and 3 of his study.

[2] *ibid.*, p. 8.

[3] Geoffrey Hawthorn, 'Explaining Human Fertility', *Sociology*, vol. 2, no. 1, Jan. 1968. See also below, p. 123.

[4] *ibid.*, p. 66.

'accounting model', for the survey is nothing more than a technique which can be used in the context of any model. Furthermore, as D. V. Glass says in connection with population studies: 'Few would argue that the mass collection of data . . . is likely to be profitable unless there are some guiding purposes in the collection'.[1] But Glass emphasizes the need for accurate data, and B. Benjamin, writing also on population research, shows that 'In order to assess the pace and direction of changes in family building it is necessary to possess serial sets of fertility rates by age at marriage, calendar year of marriage, and duration of marriage, and, if possible, by birth order'.[2] It should be obvious that a complex analysis of fertility in contemporary society is not feasible without the use of the survey technique. This is not to deny the paramount need for sociological theory to guide sociological research, including in the field of demography.

We have implied above that the principles involved in survey techniques must be rigorously observed, as indeed they have been in many studies. But misleading results may accrue not only where such principles are lightly taken, but also where inadequate preparation has been made by the researcher for undertaking the fieldwork. It is not often that studies reveal much about such preparation. There is one study, however, which furnishes an example of care taken in this connection. Thus, James Robb, who studied anti-semitism among working-class people in Bethnal Green, has drawn attention to several important preparatory tasks. First, in order to become thoroughly acquainted with the area and the people, he took up a job as a barman in the locality. Secondly, he learned the language of the district. This was invaluable for the understanding of statements made to him

[1] D. V. Glass and D. E. C. Eversley (eds.), *Population in History*, Edward Arnold, 1965, p. 5.

[2] B. Benjamin, 'The Population Census as a Source of Social Statistics', in Welford *et al., op. cit.*, p. 35.

while interviewing. As he says: 'An East Londoner, who is accustomed to expressing himself in abbreviated forms of rhyming slang, will not lapse into the Queen's English just because he is being interviewed'. Thirdly, he used an oblique approach to prepare the ground for the interview proper concerning his topic of interest. Thus he started out by a conversation about some general matters, carrying on until the Jews 'cropped up'.[1] It is clear that the researcher must display a high degree of sensitivity regarding the preparations and adjustments necessary when using certain techniques such as interviewing and observation for carrying out a field investigation.

There is another aspect of sociological research technique which requires comment. Where surveys are used—and the impression one gains is that they are becoming widespread[2] —quantification is usually involved, although not always so. This leads us directly to the question of the place of mathematics in sociology, and particularly in the analysis of empirical data. We have already mentioned the problems connected for instance with the use of statistical tests of significance.[3] On this as well as more generally, sociologists are divided. Whilst James Coleman argues that mathematics 'becomes essential as sociology moves toward the analysis of complex systems and predictions based on extended chains of deductions',[4] Aaron Cicourel points out the difficulties which arise in the very use of numerical categories and procedures, for these 'are external both to the observable social world empirically described by sociologists and to the *conceptualiza-*

---

[1] James H. Robb, *Working-Class Anti-Semite*, Tavistock, 1954, see pp. 42, 43, and foreword by W. J. H. Sprott, pp. vi–vii.

[2] See above, p. 67.

[3] See above, p. 89f.

[4] James S. Coleman, *Mathematical Sociology*, Free Press, Glencoe, Illinois, 1964, p. vii.

tions based upon these descriptions'.[1] Cicourel demands that more attention be paid to this basic problem that current research techniques involving measurement present. Notwithstanding these problems, recent advances in computer techniques have thrust mathematics further into the sociological research arena. The reason for this can be found in Geoffrey Hawthorn's observation that 'one of the problems bedevilling empirical research has always been that there are so many possible factors influencing any action . . . computer techniques have provided the tools for handling more than two or three of these at any one time in a rigorous way'.[2] As Hawthorn says, and as our review of research techniques used suggests, the more sophisticated tools, such as regression analysis, which computers make possible are as yet seldom used by sociologists. Hawthorn seems, however, content to find that many sociologists at least ask interesting questions and give plausible answers even if these are not based on rigorous research techniques. But we must move away from the stage of what could be called 'relevant speculation' and attempt to test hypotheses and prove theories by a more truly scientific approach. This is not to be interpreted, however, as a plea for nothing but quantifications, the use of statistical calculations and of computers. For there is the danger that quantitative results reify the events studied.[3] And, as Bryan Wilson fears, the price to be paid for impeccable research at a technical level, through computer development, may be puerile work 'in terms of the philosophical assumptions on which it rests' and the straightjacketing of

[1] Aaron V. Cicourel, *Method and Measurement in Sociology*, Free Press, 1964, p. 2.
[2] Geoffrey Hawthorn, 'Sociology', in Klaus Boehm (ed.), *University Choice*, Penguin, 1966, pp. 340–1.
[3] Cicourel, *op. cit.*, p. 224.

research to suit the computer.[1] The worst studies are, of course, those which apply such techniques indiscriminately, even when neither the nature of the topic nor the scale of the investigation warrants it. Research results thus obtained may be totally misleading. There are many tools that have to be employed, including those which deal with unquantifiable data, and applied in the appropriate manner, and in the research conditions where they fit, they can all help to ensure the reliability of the results.

Our final comment regarding the British studies we have reviewed is that although most of the reports contain some account of the main steps taken to carry out the investigation, we found usually little information about what went wrong during the project. Fuller 'research chronicles'[2] giving the changes made in the original aims, the reasons for the reorientations, the wrong interpretations which were made and the way these were detected and then corrected, and so on, would have given us a better understanding of the problems and pitfalls of sociological research. In this way the studies would have contributed not only to substantive knowledge regarding the investigated topics, but also to the building up and improvement of methodology in our discipline.

[1] Bryan R. Wilson, 'Analytical Studies of Social Institutions', in Welford *et al.*, *op. cit.*, p. 107.

[2] See, for instance, the 'research chronicles' given in P. E. Hammond (ed.), *Sociologists at Work*: *Essays on the Craft of Social Research*, Basic Books, New York, 1964.

4. Results

In Chapters 2 and 3 the studies referred to were used mainly for illustrative purposes; there was no attempt to include even a representative selection of material. Here, however, we shall try to provide a coherent account of the main findings in sociological research. This still does not imply a full analysis. The field is vast and, quite apart from the colossal task of writing a comprehensive report on results, since our aim is to indicate only the main trends, a fuller report would not have added anything of much value here.[1] Although the sections that follow do not treat fully the areas which they represent, they do bring together the principal findings of fields in which a substantial amount of research has been carried out.[2] At the same time the lacunae of research in some other areas, such as the sociology of art and literature,[3] the sociological study of small groups[4] or of warfare and military organization[5] is emphasized by the absence of such

[1] This is not to say that such a full report is not overdue and that it would not be valuable in itself.

[2] Regarding the theoretical orientation underlying the presentation of the material in these sections, see above, p. 17.

[3] But there has been some work in this field. See, for instance, Diana F. Laurenson, 'The Social Situation of British Writers 1860–1910', unpbl. PH.D. thesis, Univ. of London, 1966.

[4] Again a certain amount of work has been carried out in this field, but on the whole, as Bryan Wilson points out, studies of small groups have been neglected by British sociologists. See his 'A Sociologist's Footnote', in Margaret Phillips, *Small Social Groups in England*, Methuen, 1965, p. 292.

[5] There is some literature here, too, e.g. S. Andreski, *Military Organization and Society*, Routledge, 1954; and Arthur Marwick, *Britain in the Century of Total War*, Bodley Head, 1968.

material in the review which follows. Finally, the results are presented without any consideration of their utilization or practical consequences. This is an important aspect dealt with recently by R. G. Stansfield.[1] It would appear from his paper that on the whole sociological research findings are likely to make their effect felt through a slow process of 'permeation',[2] by spreading new ideas among those engaged on practical tasks. Some of the effects may even go unnoticed; they may be indirect and sometimes unintended. Under such circumstances it is clear that the evaluation of sociological research from the point of view of practical utilization is a very difficult task, requiring a sophisticated technique of cost-benefit analysis. This is a special field which will need much more attention in the future.

COMMUNITY STUDIES

In the sphere of community studies some of the prevalent beliefs were qualified by the findings. Thus, Willmott and Young point out that although families are more often on their own in the middle-class dormitory suburb than in the East End, and despite other differences between the districts, there are some similarities between them. According to the authors the bond between mother and married daughter is still strong in the suburb, but not quite to the same degree as in the city. Most old people are cared for in the suburb but special problems do exist there.[3] In a different study Willmott

[1] R. G. Stansfield, 'The Unnoticed Application of the Results of Research', paper presented at the British Association for the Advancement of Science, section N: sociology, 1 Sept. 1967.

[2] See in particular the distinction Stansfield makes between the 'package' model and the 'permeation' model for tracing the practical effects of research, *ibid.*, p. 27.

[3] Willmott and Young, *Family and Class in a London Suburb, op. cit.*, p. 123ff.

comes to the conclusion that when the time perspective is applied it will be seen that new surroundings will often allow old ways to reappear. Thus, regarding the comparative work he carried out in Dagenham, a new estate, and the 'traditional' working-class community, he says: 'At the end one is impressed how similar, not how different, they are. Local extended families, which hold such a central place in the older districts, have grown up in almost identical form on the estate, and so have local networks of neighbours. . . . In people's attitudes to their fellows, their feelings about social status and class, their political loyalties, again are close parallels between the two districts. In part Dagenham is the East End reborn'.[1]

Concerning the social problems of new communities, problems which J. H. Nicholson considers generally from the point of view of the necessary adjustments,[2] one of the important conclusions reached is that social development in such places depends on physical planning and the selection of the original population. The importance of adequate physical conditions, particularly for the younger generations, is brought out by Vereker and Mays in their study of attitudes to mobility in an old decaying central city district. They say that many of the younger residents consider the conditions there as unsatisfactory and, therefore, 'they wish either to leave such neighbourhoods entirely or would require them to be drastically rebuilt and refurbished with a variety of amenities that at present are seen to be lacking'. Another of their conclusions is that 'The warm contact emanating from the intimate social groups and from the extended family in particular is clearly deemed by many people to be less important than the opportunity to enjoy the advantages of better physical and social conditions'.[3] H. E. Bracey's study also points to the apparently

[1] Willmott, *The Evolution of a Community, op. cit.*, p. 109.
[2] *op. cit.*, p. 15.
[3] Vereker and Mays, *op. cit.*, pp. 118–19.

increasing demand for adequate social amenities. As he says, 'The message of [his] enquiry demands for bigger, better and more comprehensive patterns of social activity and participation'.[1]

Population mobility, which was given attention by Vereker and Mays, Willmott and Young, Nicholson and others, raises not only problems of physical and social amenities, changes in family ties and the care for the old, but may in certain circumstances bring about a conflict situation which could split the community. In this connection Margaret Stacey's findings are interesting. The conclusion that emerges from her study is that Banbury's problem was not so much that of having to absorb a new influx of people but that it had to face the challenge to the local tradition. This challenge was symbolized by the new ideas and ways of life that the workers of the newly established factory in this locality had brought with them. According to Stacey, Banbury ceased to be *one* community although it might later develop into one entity. But this would not be in full sense because of the new complexity and the fact that it is closely integrated with the wider English society. The implications of this are that 'Change is loosening the ties of the in-turning traditional society and reducing the intensity of local relationships'.[2]

Having set out some of the conclusions of studies dealing with local communities we shall now turn to two more general surveys, one encompassing London and the other the towns of England and Wales. One of the merits of the study of London by the Centre for Urban Studies is that it continues the work of the earlier surveys, that is of Charles Booth at the end of the last century and the New London Survey of the 1930s.

The papers in the symposium provide us with useful

---

[1] *op. cit.*, p. 190ff.
[2] Stacey, *op. cit.*, p. 177.

insights into the trends in metropolitan growth and the contemporary structure of Greater London. But the results of the surveys of some of the new communities are particularly interesting, in that these, too, as the other studies mentioned above, emphasize the importance of linking up physical with social planning. Thus Ruth Glass in her introduction says: 'The three surveys (Lansbury, South Oxhey and Pimlico) show that even in the confident post-war days, town planning—by definition a deliberate, rational pursuit—tended to be afflicted by the hangover of haphazard, arbitrary, out-dated ideas and procedures. And while these reports present examples of the considerable achievements of municipal enterprise, they also confirm that town planning, by itself, is a misnomer: without the backing of comprehensive social and economic planning, it is bound to be rather slow and incoherent, and it is not likely to go very far. Nor has it gone very far: since the mid-fifties, "planning" has been compelled to retreat'.[1]

The more specialized studies presented so far, including the ones in the symposium mentioned, give way to a generalized attempt to produce an 'urban typology' in the analysis of statistical material regarding British towns which was undertaken by Moser and Scott. Their study is important for the following reasons: 'Hitherto in this country no systematic and general research has been done into the ways in which British towns differ from or resemble one another. One is all too ready to speak of *the* urban dweller, *the* urban pattern, *the* urban way of life, without appreciating the variations found both within and between cities. Many studies have investigated differences between towns for one particular factor, such as infant mortality, in terms of other features like social class or housing conditions. The central idea of this

[1] *London—Aspects of Change*, ed. by Centre for Urban Studies, MacGibbon & Kee, 1964, p. xxxiiff.

study has been to unravel the relationships between a great
number of urban characteristics, and measure them precisely,
rather than to study in detail any single feature'.[1] Despite the
notable diversity between the towns the authors point out
that many have features in common, so that they can be
grouped. Thus, the two main categories thrown up by the
results are north and south. Moser and Scott say: 'For a large
range of characteristics, it appears almost as if there were two
universes of towns within the narrow confines of this country,
divided by a line running approximately from the Wash in
the east to the Bristol Channel in the west; leaving the
industrial towns of Durham, Yorkshire and Lancashire on
one side, and the market towns, London suburbs and
seaside resorts of southern England on the other.'[2] Of course,
the authors stress the differences between towns in the north,
the Midlands and Wales, Greater London and the south-east,
and the remainder of the south and south-west. The much
more revealing classification, however, is that arrived at by
extracting a small number of underlying factors from the mass
of data which was scrutinized. The authors discerned common
factors underlying a large number of variables. They thus
extracted four major components: (1) social class; (2) population change between 1931 and 1951; (3) population change
between 1951 and 1958; (4) overcrowding. The first component 'confirms the importance of the social class element in
urban differentiation'. Components 2 and 3 are concerned
with the town's stage of development. Thus, the analysis
shows that 'As a town grows older, and space becomes
cramped, the younger people tend to move out to new
housing estates in the suburbs, or to adjacent towns, leaving
behind them a surplus of older people. This movement is
characterized by various features, such as low average size of

[1] Moser and Scott, *op. cit.*, p. 2.
[2] *ibid.*, p. 9.

household, a preponderance of the elderly, low birth rates, houses lacking in modern conveniences, and relatively high per capita retail sales'. Attention is paid by the authors also to the 'cycle of growth' of towns. And the last component is important, for it relates to housing density and thus distinguishes towns by basic living conditions.[1]

An attempt to construct a theory of social change[2] by fitting the existing community studies into a morphological continuum, was made by Ronald Frankenberg. He used the two polar types of 'truly rural' and 'urban', and regarded the continuum as morphological 'because although each stage is structurally more complicated than the one before, and each has a more diversified economy and technology, there is no necessary implication that the village of Glynceiriog in North Wales used to be like the mid-Wales parish, Llanfihangel, and will become successively like the coal-mining town of Ashton, the Derbyshire manufacturing town Glossop, or Banbury, Bethnal Green, Watling and Sheffield'. Nevertheless, Frankenberg maintains that 'at each level of organization there are linked changes',[3] and that although different towns at one level will have their individual characteristics, both material and cultural, underlying these differences, they will have similarities in social structure and social behaviour. In elaborating his continuum Frankenberg uses 25 themes starting off with *community* and *association* as one set of poles to his continuum.[4] He does not mention Ferdinand Tonnies' dichotomy of *Gemeinschaft* and *Gesellschaft*,[5] perhaps in an attempt to free his analysis from any connection with Tonnies'

[1] *ibid.*, pp. 14, 15.
[2] See below for a discussion of the views of British sociologists regarding general theories of social change, pp. 176–84.
[3] Ronald Frankenberg, *Communities in Britain*, Penguin, 1966, p. 237.
[4] *ibid.*, p. 290.
[5] Ferdinand Tonnies, *Community and Association* (tr. from German), Routledge, 1955.

sentimentality; but in essence there is little difference between the meaning Frankenberg gives to his terms and the meaning of Tonnies' terms, i.e. close communal relationship as against contractual impersonal relationship. Frankenberg's detailed analysis goes, however, beyond description and deeply into the question of social development as evinced by community life in Britain.

There is no doubt that the studies mentioned so far constitute an important advance in our knowledge of the conditions in which people live in Britain, both physical and social, and in our understanding of community life. Furthermore, these studies have been instrumental in drawing our attention to the many changes that have been taking place in recent years and the problems that such changes have created.

THE FAMILY, THE LIFE CYCLE AND RELATED PROBLEMS

Here we shall collate the results of studies about family life, youth and its problems, old age, institutional care generally, the sociology of medicine and demography. These are not disparate aspects of societal life, but are closely linked elements reflecting the varying adjustments called for of the individual who finds himself in differing circumstances, according to his age, health and familial conditions, much of which is affected by the kind of society he lives in and the institutional arrangements and relationships in that society. This is a large area, and some of it is within the province of 'social administration'. Inevitably the area is far from covered but a sufficient number of examples are given to bring out the main sociological conclusions reached in this field.

Comparing the contemporary family with that of the period before or during the nineteenth-century development of industrialization, Ronald Fletcher says in his main conclusion that what his foregoing analysis seems to point to is that 'it is quite untrue to say that the family in contemporary Britain has been "stripped of its functions" and has, as a consequence, become of diminished importance as a social institution'. Fletcher shows in fact that the modern family fulfils *more* functions than its predecessor and that it does this in a more detailed and sophisticated manner. He upholds his conclusions as regards both senses of the sociological meaning of the term 'function', i.e. 'the human need and purposes which the institution exists to "satisfy" and the "functional intercon-nection" which the institution has with the wider network of institutions in society'. Thus he reiterates that on the one hand 'the family is now concerned with a more detailed and refined satisfaction of needs than hitherto', and on the other 'it is also more intimately and responsibly bound up with the wider and more complicated network of social institutions in the modern state than it was prior to industrialization'.[1]

O. R. McGregor and Griselda Rowntree similarly express an optimistic view regarding the contemporary family.[2] After charting the fundamental changes in family life during this century and paying particular attention to 'their impact on those parts of the law which regulate family life', they come to conclusions which dash any anxieties about the danger of the family disintegrating or its social stability being in peril. Such generalizations have been made by persons ill-informed about family life in Britain and they are contradicted by the material assembled by McGregor and Rowntree. The authors point out, however, that a great deal of work still remains to be done. 'Research has still much to contribute before a reliable assessment of the quality of present-day family life can be made. There is little empirical knowledge of the

[1] Fletcher, *op. cit.*, p. 177.
[2] O. R. McGregor and Griselda Rowntree, 'The Family', in A. T. Welford *et al.*, *Society, op. cit.*, ch. 21.

attitude to marriage in different social strata or of people's expectations of this most popular state. Such research is a pressing need, for, in the absence of knowledge, confident but baseless assertions proliferate'.[1]

The large amount of confused thinking on, for example, patterns of sexual conduct and divorce are brought to our attention by Alex Comfort[2] and O. R. McGregor[3] respectively. Again, as we shall see, both the attitudes and behaviour of young people as regards sex life have been misconstrued, promiscuity—as Schofield points out, for instance[4]—not being the accepted standard of the majority. And the Eppels have stressed that their research has made it quite clear that 'an overwhelming majority of . . . young people have a high valuation of marriage and family life'.[5]

Raymond Firth places the family in industrial society into the wider perspective of kinship relations. He brings together the available evidence[6] and comes to the conclusion that 'industrialization does not necessarily destroy or indeed radically alter the expressive sphere of . . . kin ties', but he suggests that development towards an industrial society probably does 'break down the formal structure of kin groups, except perhaps that of the elementary family, which is most resistant'.[7] Even so, Firth argues, on the strength of his own researches in north London and other available material, that

[1] *ibid*., p. 425.

[2] Alex Comfort, *Sex in Society*, Penguin, 1964, e.g. p. 116ff.

[3] O. R. McGregor, *Divorce in England*, Heinemann, 1957, p. 194ff.

[4] See below, p. 112f.

[5] E. M. and M. Eppel, *Adolescents and Morality*, Routledge, 1966, p. 219.

[6] See particularly his footnote 25, where he quotes his own *Two Studies of Kinship in London*, 1956, as well as studies by Young and Willmott, Townsend and many other British sociologists. See Raymond Firth, 'Family and Kinship in Industrial Society', *Sociological Review Monograph 8*, Keele, 1964, pp. 81, 86.

[7] *ibid*., p. 83.

in all social classes there is a similar affective quality in kin networks, although the actual operation of the network, as distinct from other underlying non-affective binding forces such as material considerations, *may* differ from class to class.[1] But as with McGregor and Rowntree his paper also ends on a note stressing the need for more sociological research, particularly empirical research, about the family and its larger kin setting.

Peter Townsend also suggests that the extended family is adjusting to new circumstances and is not disintegrating. His evidence concerns the role of the family in the lives of old people. 'To the old person as much as to the young [the family] seems to be the supreme comfort and support. Its central purpose is as strong as ever. It continues to provide a natural, if conservative, means of self-fulfilment and expression, as the individual moves from the first to the third generation, performing and teaching the functions of child, parent and grandparent'.[2]

Townsend's view is in line with the more optimistic results of gerontological research in the post-war period.[3] As Jeremy Tunstall has pointed out, these studies have shown that the stereotype of a gloomy and isolated existence in old age is an exaggerated picture, the majority adjusting well to retirement and old age, and being mobile and enjoying regular contact with their family and other relatives. Townsend himself, however, as we quote him below (p. 115), has drawn attention to the existing unsatisfactory conditions for the large majority of old people who live in institutions, whilst Tunstall concentrated his attention on a smaller section of old people who live alone and whom he found to be isolated.[4] In delving deeper into the phenomenon of isolation among some old

---

[1] *ibid.*, pp. 84, 85.
[2] *op. cit.*, p. 210.
[3] See Jeremy Tunstall, *Old and Alone*, Routledge, 1966, p. 2.
[4] *ibid.*, p. 245.

people Tunstall recognizes both that personality factors may be important in predisposing some to isolation and also that special personality adjustment is required of the old person who finds himself in a socially isolated situation. It appears that longitudinal studies of middle-aged and elderly people as they get older would be needed, for, as Tunstall points out, two basic complexities must be recognized: 'firstly, patterns of aging stretch far back into the individual's past, and secondly, there is a great variety in social relations in old age'.[1]

Dealing with the position of youth in contemporary society, we must first and foremost draw attention to the factual results of a survey which helps to dispel many misconceptions and exaggerated generalizations about young people. This is particularly useful since the study is in one of the areas where biased views abound. Thus Michael Schofield's survey results suggest that 'promiscuity, although it exists, is not a prominent feature of teenage sexual behaviour. Consequently the risks of venereal disease are not very great, and this conclusion is supported by the figures'.[2] It is true that 'promiscuity' was defined as sexual intercourse with several partners over a certain period of time rather than just indulgence in sexual intercourse with one partner. But it is the former which is most dangerous for the spread of diseases.[3] Furthermore, Schofield also came up with figures which show that sex relations among teenagers were not as common as believed. He says that the 'results have made it clear that pre-marital sexual relations are a long way from being universal among teenagers as over two-thirds of the boys and three-quarters of the girls in [the] sample have not engaged in sexual intercourse'. He also points out, however, that 'it is equally apparent that teenage pre-marital intercourse is not a minority

[1] *ibid.*, pp. 246, 268.
[2] *op. cit.*, p. 253.
[3] *ibid.*, foreword by Sir Herbert Broadley, p. vii.

problem confined to a few deviates. It is an activity common enough to be seen as one manifestation of teenage conformity'.[1]

In a specialized field of research about the domestic and social consequences of women working on full-time shifts C. R. Hutton's conclusions are important. The family was found to be small, but young children were adequately supervised in the mother's absence. Although the undertaking of work was found to be popular, there was a high rate of absence and the job as such was regarded as no more than one phase in these women's working lives.[2] In yet another study of the family, this time from the aspect of behaviour patterns within it, the conclusions reached are as follows. Both husband and wife showed strong tendencies towards joint activity and more than half of the activity/power patterns were found to be of a cooperative nature. Of equal, if not greater, importance are the suggestions made as to possible areas of further investigation. Thus, Baskerville, who carried out this research, puts forward the following suggestions: (a) the preparation of an adequate scale for measuring tasks and decisions within the household; (b) an investigation of the trends in home centredness and cooperative family activities; and (c) a comparative study of the way in which middle-class families make new social contacts on different kinds of housing estate.[3]

Important insights have been provided by a number of studies regarding the problem of role-playing on behalf of family members and the way this affects their lives and that of the family. Thus, Hannah Gavron found a role conflict in the lives of married women with young children, who when

---

[1] *ibid.*, p. 248.
[2] Caroline R. Hutton, 'Married Women on Full-Time Shiftwork', unpbl. M.A. thesis, Univ. of London, 1962. It is interesting that, compared with modern times, the working mother of the Victorian era did show child neglect: see Margaret Hewitt, *Wives and Mothers in Victorian Industry*, Rockliff, 1958.
[3] D. R. Baskerville, *op. cit.*

of working-class background lack the opportunities of either an emancipated life, which they had been taught to expect, or a 'woman's world', because those who have no young children go out to work—hence they must remain reconciled to their roles as mothers. The consequences are that whilst the middle-class wife pursues interests independent of her domestic roles, the working-class wife tries to make the husband share in her domestic roles.[1] Another kind of role duality was highlighted by Viola Klein. This concerns women's functions both as workers and as wives and mothers. The conclusion reached in this study suggests that adjustments, especially on the employment side, have been insufficient to allow women to perform both their functions well and at the same time not to affect adversely either their homes or jobs.[2] Finally, in connection with problem families A. F. Philp emphasizes the difficulties that arise in some of the families in which there is an unsatisfactory execution of the 'male role'.[3]

Pauline Morris found that the effect on the family of the loss of the male head, through the latter's imprisonment, was not the sole cause of problems, but she concluded that imprisonment did aggravate the situation.[4] With regard to the specific hypotheses tested she found convincing evidence only for two of the five hypotheses set up,[5] namely, that the same pattern of family relationship will follow imprisonment as preceded it, and that during the husband's imprisonment the wives with wide kinship networks will seek additional support from them.[6] On the whole, little relationship was found between the environmental factors of the family and the adjustment to separation.[7]

[1] Gavron, *op. cit.*
[2] Klein, *op. cit.*, p. 134ff.
[3] Philp, *op. cit.*, p. 275ff.
[4] Morris, *op. cit.*, pp. 9, 11.
[5] See above, p. 27.
[6] *op. cit.*, p. 302.
[7] *ibid.*, p. 225.

A few examples will be given here of the results of research in the field of social services. Naturally most of these studies are connected with some aspect of family life. E. M. Wilson considered the family welfare services in two new towns and came to the following conclusions. The deficiencies of the services investigated lay in the existence of administrative and geographical hindrances, a shortage of properly trained staff, inadequate coordination of various services and the lack of 'family-centred services'.[1] In a study of the success and failure of foster-home placements R. E. Parker was able to draw up a predictive table which was tested and the findings of which were validated by the test.[2] As regards, for instance, the problems of hospitalization, the main findings of Ann Cartwright reinforce Titmuss' views which pinpointed the clash between the tendency to run institutions in the interests of their staff and the need to pay more attention to the needs of those for whom they care.[3] Enid Mills, dealing with the care of the mentally ill, highlights the confusion regarding the services provided for such persons and, as in the case of the family welfare services, in one of her main findings stresses the need for some rationalization.[4] Regarding the long report of Peter Townsend on the institutional care of old people, 'so far as it is possible to express in a few words the general conclusion [of that report] it is that communal Homes of the kind which exist in England and Wales today do not adequately meet the physical, psychological and social needs of the elderly people living in them, and that alternative services and living arrangements should quickly take their place'.[5]

[1] Elaine M. Wilson, 'Family Welfare Services in the New Towns of Harlow and Stevenage', unpbl. M.A. thesis, Univ. of London, 1962.

[2] R. A. Parker, 'The Application of Predictive Techniques to the Practice of Social Work', unpbl. PH.D. thesis, Univ. of London, 1961.

[3] Cartwright, *op. cit.*, p. 204ff, and R. M. Titmuss, *op. cit.*, p. 122.

[4] Mills, *op. cit.*, p. 146ff.

[5] Peter Townsend, *The Last Refuge*, p. 430. See also P. Townsend and D. Wedderburn, *The Aged in the Welfare State*, Bell, 1965.

Whether of a specific or more general nature, the studies concerned with social services have produced results which can be usefully employed to improve the services.

A number of the foregoing studies show how we impinge on the questions of the relationship between medicine and the social sciences. An interesting symposium[1] has brought together a fair number of papers dealing with the general area, and including specific topics such as 'Hospital Attitudes and Communications',[2] 'Sociological and Social-psychological Issues of the Out-patient Clinic',[3] and 'Some Medical and Social Characteristics of Elderly People under State Care'.[4] Perhaps the most interesting conclusions in the symposium are those by John Simpson who deals with research priorities in the medico-sociological field.[5] It has been pointed out by other writers such as Susser and Watson that the social environment as well as the physical environment has its effect on the causes and outcome of disease,[6] but Simpson claims that although the psychiatrist has accepted the role of social science for understanding mental illness, physicians in other branches of clinical medicine 'have yet to be convinced that the social sciences can contribute significantly to the proper understanding of infectious, degenerative, traumatic, toxic, metabolic and neophastic diseases that constitute the bulk of human illness'. This field awaits much more exploration but Simpson shows that some studies already give important leads regarding the ecological aspects of physical illness. These are some of the preliminary conclusions: (a) sickness is not uniformly distributed in the population—'most of the

---

[1] 'Sociology and Medicine', *Sociological Review Monograph 5*, Keele, 1962.

[2] *ibid.*, paper by R. W. Revans.

[3] *ibid.*, paper by G. M. Carstairs and J. G. Bruhn.

[4] *ibid.*, paper by D. Kay, P. Beamish and Martin Roth.

[5] *ibid.*, paper by John Simpson.

[6] M. W. Susser and W. Watson, *Sociology in Medicine, op. cit.*

illnesses in the active population appear to be concentrated in a small proportion of its membership'; (b) socio-economic class has some influence on the frequency of illness; (c) 'adverse childhood experiences are positively correlated with adult ill-health'. These and other pieces of evidence, such as experimental studies showing that the reaction of the human being to his social environment involves adaptations which lead to bodily processes that are mediated through neural or hormonal influences, make it clear to Simpson that 'Man's interaction with his social and interpersonal environment is relevant, therefore, not merely to his emotional state or to his mental health but to all the illness that he experiences'. This is, then, a large field where research would be rewarding. Similarly Main and Papoport highlight the possibilities and special features of research in 'hospital sociology', where experimental situations are more easily given than in most other sociological research, where there is fairly easy access to important materials about personal and family details, but where the crisis element also means that work must be carried out in trying situations.[1]

Looking at studies about youth in general the main conclusions seem to be: that 'the maturational and social phase we call youth' presents certain problems, that the chief among these problems is 'the cleavage between the generations'.[2] According to Mays the exaggerated way in which differences between the generations is perceived by the adult world leads to alienation or 'a state of cultural *anomie*'. A similar point is brought out by the Eppels, who focused particularly on the values of young people. The upshot of their enquiry is that the younger generation resent the lack of understanding of the older generation. To aggravate this inter-generation hostility the adolescents feel that they are

[1] T. F. Main and R. N. Rapoport, 'Hospital Sociology', in A. T. Welford *et al.*, *op. cit.*, p. 567.

[2] J. B. Mays, *The Young Pretenders*, Michael Joseph, 1965, p. 165.

under attack, and the authors assure us that there is 'plenty of evidence from an analysis of the climate of opinion that their feeling of being under attack and in an embattled situation has some justification in reality'.[1] This alienated position has led them to use the quality of personal relationships in their assessment of people's moral standards and to regard traditional sanction as of less importance. Despite this, the Eppels maintain that 'they have not rejected the general ethic . . . but are groping for new sanctions', and that there is 'a genuine concern with moral problems and moral conflict'.[2]

Musgrove's study also points at a different conflict situation. This is that, on the one hand, 'with the expansion of higher education, far more of the young men are well qualified for the senior posts which are now less quickly vacated',[3] whilst on the other hand, 'when . . . the author attempted to discover the attitude of adults towards the earlier entry of adolescents into adult life, he found an overwhelming rejection of the idea, but a general agreement that adolescents should inhabit a segregated and virtually autonomous, non-adult social sphere'.[4] Considering the impact of education on the younger generation from the completely different angle of religious identification Joan Brothers found that 'the old devotion and loyalty to the parochial settings have come to have little meaning to most of these young people who have attended grammar schools'.[5] Brothers maintains that from the point of view of the Catholic religion this younger generation cannot be regarded as uprooted. It is merely that they have a more abstract concept of the Church which results in an identification with it that goes beyond the local setting. Considering this, the importance of Brothers' research lies in that her

[1] E. M. and M. Eppel, *op. cit.*, p. 213.
[2] *ibid.*, pp. 215, 218.
[3] F. Musgrove, *Youth and the Social Order*, Routledge, 1964, p. 163.
[4] *ibid.*, pp. 11, 12.
[5] *op. cit.*, p. 159.

findings 'reveal the inability of the parochial structure, as is currently understood by clergy and people in Liverpool, to absorb the impact of new attitudes and ideas'.

The results of all these studies suggest that major reorientations are necessary in many spheres where new educational trends are bringing about changes in the lives of the rising generations. Without the necessary adjustments, particularly on behalf of the traditionally attached sectors of society, conflicts are likely to arise.

Demographic studies provide us with another important slant on family and the life cycle; the study of population fluctuations, the main concern of demography, is obviously directly related to family life where birth rates are concerned, and to the life cycle where death rates are concerned (a third factor, the balance between emigration and immigration, is also important in some cases). Many demographers, such as D. V. Glass and D. E. C. Eversley, stress that these factors must be seen in the wider context of society and historical antecedents. In fusing together the views of a number of writers Glass states that 'population theory cannot be discussed without reference to the nature of a particular society',[1] and elsewhere Eversley concludes that a sociological framework can be used, for instance, in starting off investigations regarding fertility patterns in a given society.[2]

A sociological framework was in fact used by J. A. and O. Banks who studied family planning in Victorian England. Their hypothesis, concerned with the influence of feminism on family planning, concluded that 'from the literature at our disposal there is no evidence that "emancipated" women in the feminist sense of the term, once married, had fewer children than those in the same social class who were "unemancipated", although they were, in the early years of

[1] D. V. Glass (ed.), *Introduction to Malthus*, Watts, 1953, p. x.
[2] D. E. C. Eversley, *Social Theories of Fertility and the Malthusian Debate*, Clarendon Press, Oxford, 1959, p. 272.

feminism, more likely to stay unmarried'. Further, the authors point out that family planning was established within the middle-class at a time when feminism as an organized movement was still developing. They also say that 'all evidence points to the initiative in the matter being taken by the man in a society largely dominated by masculine values'.[1] And this initiative was taken as a result of economic considerations. This research by J. A. and Olive Banks presents a case-study of the relationship between social movements and social change. The study provides an excellent example of the careful setting up of an hypothesis,[2] of the skilful use and handling of available secondary material, of the drawing of clear conclusions and of using this for prediction and advice for those setting out social policy elsewhere, as for instance in over-populated developing countries. Economic conditions, technology, religious affiliations, wars, hygiene and medical developments, as well as other factors, contribute to the quantity and quality of a population. These variables and their interrelationships can best be analysed through the framework of society, and the need for such an approach can be seen in research concerned with historical demography.[3] The important perspective to arise from these points is that, as E. Grebenik says, whilst demography is concerned with numbers of populations, the division of populations into subgroups by sex, age and marital status and the changes in these, it is also 'taken to include the study of long-term population movements and theoretical speculations about the causes of such movements'.[4]

[1] J. A. and Olive Banks, *op. cit.*, p. 130.
[2] See above, p. 27, as well as the whole introduction of the authors, esp. p. vii.
[3] See D. V. Glass and D. E. C. Eversley (eds.), *Population in History*, Edward Arnold, 1965.
[4] E. Grebenik, 'Demography', in Gould and Kolb (eds.), *Dictionary of the Social Sciences, op. cit.*, p. 188.

Both speculations about past changes and guessing—if possible accurately projecting—future changes are important, for population change has many social implications. Kelsall points to a few of these, including problems of aging, housing and migration.[1] Another of the implications mentioned by Kelsall is the changing role of middle-aged married women. Thus, 'the tendency to marry younger, the broad trend towards smaller families and the increased expectation of life, have between them meant that today's married woman is free of family-building and family-rearing responsibilities much earlier',[2] and this together with the easier task of running a home in the technological society has had the effect of releasing a large number of women for more work outside the home and for more leisure activities. The question which then arises is whether these women can play a full part in their community with their changed role, i.e. whether the necessary employment and leisure opportunities are held out to them.[3]

To be able to meet the contingencies due to impending changes it must be possible to predict the latter fairly accurately. But despite much research effort in this field the predictions tend to be shaky. The unforeseen circumstances that may affect fertility and migration and even mortality are many and varied. Furthermore, the necessary information has not always been available. Thus, Glass and Grebenik, commenting on fertility trends in Britain, found that national statistics were deficient for such predictive purposes.[4] On the same issue Kelsall says: 'It is on the family-building side

---

[1] R. K. Kelsall, *Population*, Longmans, 1967, chs. 8 and 9.

[2] *ibid.*, p. 58.

[3] *ibid.*, p. 59.

[4] D. V. Glass and E. Grebenik, summary chapter from *Trend and Pattern of Fertility in Great Britain* (Report of the Family Census, 1946), HMSO, 1954, p. 12; and see Royal Commission on Population, papers, vol. 6.

that both our knowledge as to why people act as they do and the means of persuading them to modify their action, seem to be at their weakest. It is no secret, for example, that the "boom in babies" in 1956 and subsequent years came as a complete surprise to demographers and others. No one had forecast a development of this kind on this scale, and *ex-post-facto* explanations as to why it happened, and as to the chances of the trend either continuing or being reversed, are by no means convincing'. Therefore, Kelsall urges that 'a major programme of research is clearly needed both into the factors influencing parents in their family building and into the probable effects of different measures of state policy'.[1] John Boreham had already suggested some factors of state policy and other conditions that might have caused the increase: 'The introduction of family allowances, the increase of child allowances for income tax, the extensions of social security benefits of all sorts, the absence of economic slumps of the pre-war intensity, the slow but steady increase in real incomes and the influx of immigrants'.[2] He is uncertain, however why the increase should have been so sudden in the mid-1950s. In the light of this uncertainty it is quite clear why P. R. Cox singled out 'fertility' as one of a few areas where further research was needed.[3]

Despite the uncertainty some attempt at forecasting fertility has been made. It is in terms of a continuing but slower rise, a prediction backed up by the following factors likely to be at work; a continuing rise in real per capita income, improved standards in housing, the fashion for larger families, the falling age of puberty, the possibility that the recent increase was in part due to immigration and the possible effects of

[1] Kelsall, *op. cit.*, p. 94.
[2] John Boreham, 'The Pressure of Population', *New Society*, 3 March 1966, p. 10.
[3] Peter R. Cox, *Demography*, C.U.P., 1959, pp. 331–3.

simpler and more effective contraceptive methods.[1] In areas other than actual fertility trends, short-run predictions can be made with greater certainty. One example, given by Boreham. is that of estimating the size of future school and university populations, and hence enabling those planning such services to meet future demands. The complex relationship between population trends, the general social structure and social policy is clear testimony to the need for the sociological perspective in the field of demography.

This need is stressed in a recent paper by Geoffrey Hawthorn, who feels that the absence of a proper sociological theory in the study of human fertility is fully responsible for lack of progress in this field over the last decade and a half— for instance, the inability to provide accurate fertility predictions. Hawthorn attacks the rise of the survey in fertility studies on the ground apparently that this means accepting a simplified model of causality which singles out inventory-fashion only certain factors for analysis; and he proposes to replace it by a broader model, similar to the Malthusian theory, i.e. that populations are self-regulating by force of desire for survival. 'From what I have already said about explanations of population size and change, it would seem to follow that the only acceptable explanatory model would be one which took all the factors into account with some notion of equilibrium'. This, he says, 'should be a model in which the idea of equilibrium is used as an assumption, in that it is maintained that, say, a population is working towards an equilibrium with its environment'.[2] Hawthorn's 'ideal' model may well be the kind of theoretical push that fertility studies need, but it is argued above (p. 96) that he erroneously counterpoises this model to the survey technique. On the

[1] Boreham, *op. cit.*
[2] Geoffrey Hawthorn, 'Explaining Human Fertility', *Sociology*, vol. 2, no. 1, Jan. 1968, p. 71ff.

whole, however, Hawthorn reflects the greater awareness which has been developing regarding the need for sociological theory to guide demographic research.

EDUCATION/MASS COMMUNICATION

The results emanating from the field of the sociology of education point to various conflict situations. One such situation concerns the student with working-class or middle-class background. Peter Marris points out that university education prepares for elite membership by reserving the most prestige-conferring careers for successful graduates. But half the students he surveyed were children of fathers who did not have occupations with such high social standing. And he concludes that 'If occupation and education remain . . . crucial determinants of distinctive styles of life and values, these students were faced with a conflict between their background and their probable future. A university degree would force them to reinterpret where they stood in terms of social stratification. They could hardly enjoy all the opportunities their education offered without in part repudiating the society in which they grew up, and so disparaging their own roots'.[1] This poses a dilemma and, according to Marris, partly explains the detachment from political issues characteristic of the students he surveyed. The detachment 'helps to exclude the social differences that elsewhere constrain relationships, and releases intellectual inquiry from concern with immediate limitations on its practicality'. Marris sees this detachment as producing a risk in that it 'will foster a culture so autonomous as to be no longer integrated with the society which sustains it'.[2]

[1] P. Marris, *The Experience of Higher Education*, Routledge, 1964, p. 153.
[2] *ibid.*, p. 165.

The conflict between theory and practice, or rather the discrepancies between the way the whole educational system was envisaged to work and how in fact it turned out to work are highlighted by many studies. As we pointed out in Chapter 2, much of the post-war research in this field concentrated upon the relationship between social class and educational opportunity.[1] The results of these researches all point to the educational system itself as well as environmental factors working against the child who comes from lower social classes. Some of the findings may be set out as follows: (a) Olive Banks contends that 'the arguments used against the tripartite system and in favour of the multilateral approach are . . . sound'. She points out that 'if the prestige of a school derives [as it does in practice] from the social and economic status of the occupation for which it prepares, then equality of prestige is clearly impossible', as was originally envisaged for the three types of secondary education.[2] (b) Jackson and Marsden argue that the educational system on the whole works against valuable working-class elements of the national culture being transmitted and fostered, a factor which favours the middle class, and forces those below to accommodate to its values.[3] (c) Again Jackson shows that streaming in primary education produced a system for 'cutting down talent in the hunt for the chosen few'.[4] (d) Official reports show clearly how the system permits the waste of a very large pool of ability.[5] (e) Floud and others found in their study of Middlesbrough and south-west Hertfordshire that class inequalities, although somewhat reduced, persisted in regard to the relation between

[1] See above, p. 28.

[2] Olive Banks, *Parity and Prestige in English Secondary Education*, Routledge, 1955, p. 243.

[3] Jackson and Marsden, *op. cit.*, p. 243.

[4] Jackson, *op. cit.*, and Jackson and Marsden, *op. cit.*, p. 248.

[5] See *Early Leaving*, Central Advisory Council for Education, 1954; *15–18* (Crowther Report), 1959; *Higher Education* (Robbins Report), appendix 1.

ability and opportunity to enter grammar schools.[1] (f) But the measuring of ability itself, e.g. through IQ tests, is likely to be influenced by social factors such as class, as Bernstein's work on linguistic development showed.[2] (g) Inferior environmental factors such as found in a slum district of Liverpool also cause disadvantages to one section of the population, as J. B. Mays showed.[3] (h) Douglas' national sample proved beyond doubt that at every single stage of his schooling the working-class child was at a disadvantage through poorer home conditions and other factors.[4]

M. B. Gaine, who reviewed the literature in some detail, concludes thus: 'All the evidence which has accumulated over the last twenty years points to the fact that the 1944 Education Act did not achieve one of the principal purposes for which it was designed: to provide equality of educational opportunity for all. Where fifty years ago the social reformers were seeking to remove the barriers to *educational opportunity* by providing free places and scholarships, it is now realised that there are social barriers to *educability*, and it is not at all clear that administrative changes in the structure of education will be sufficient to remove these barriers'.[5] Such conclusions were foreseeable in the light of the investigations carried out, in the period shortly after the Second World War, by David Glass and his associates. The latter considered the factor of education within the broader process of social mobility and came to the conclusions that 'the type and level of education attained . . . depended very heavily upon the social status

[1] J. E. Floud *et al.*, *op. cit.*

[2] B. Bernstein, 'Social Class: Speech Systems and Psycho-therapy', *British Journal of Sociology*, vol. 15, no. 1, March 1964, p. 56; see also his article 'A Public Language: Some Sociological Implications', *British Journal of Sociology*, vol. 10, no. 4, Dec. 1959.

[3] J. B. Mays, *Growing up in the City*, *op. cit.*

[4] J. W. B. Douglas, *op. cit.*

[5] M. B. Gaine, 'Sociology and Education', in J. D. Halloran and Joan Brothers (eds.), *Uses of Sociology*, Sheed & Ward, 1966, p. 151.

(as measured in terms of occupation) of the subjects' fathers'; and that 'taking male subjects only, the relation between parental and filial status was seen to be positive and significant at all levels of the status hierarchy, and especially high at the upper levels'.[1] The investigations directed by Glass, and the other contributions in this field, have provided us with a clearer picture of the link between the institutional order of education and social stratification.

In this section our account of research results extends beyond that of the field of formal education. This is necessary for two reasons, both of which are mentioned by J. M. Trenaman. First, in the modern society of Britain the new media of mass communication have within recent years expanded to a remarkable degree. Thus, 'In the space of only a few years, the new informal media have far outstripped in extent of communication the traditional methods of the class tutor', a fact that Trenaman considers to be a revolution in communication no less significant socially than the invention of writing or printing.[2] Secondly, as Trenaman shows, early formal education strongly influences the selection of different kinds and qualities of communication and culture within the population. In one of his studies the sample population divided rather equally between those who were interested in new ideas, learning and the acquisition of knowledge, and those who were resistant to new ideas and higher values. The former group tended to have good education and were mainly in skilled occupations. And their greater interest in knowledge and learning was revealed by the fact that they tended to

[1] D. V. Glass (ed.), *Social Mobility in Britain*, Routledge, 1954, p. 291. It should be noted that although a good deal of this volume is given to the relationship between education and social mobility, the studies brought together cover a far wider field, pertinent to the study of social differentiation and mobility, and the volume also deals in detail with technical aspects of research in these areas.

[2] J. M. Trenaman, *Communication and Comprehension*, Longmans, 1967, p. 185ff.

'listen or look at the more serious programmes, usually read the more responsible items in their newspapers (and were) often members of the public library'.[1] Furthermore, going up the educational scale, interests and knowledge extend and proliferate, and the general picture gained is one of an educationally stratified society in a pyramidal shape, 'rich and complex at the top, impoverished at the bottom'.[2] This educational and cultural division of society is perpetuated by the selection process for educational opportunities and the differential chances for social mobility resulting in two widely differing cultural value systems. In Richard Hoggart's terms we have the working-class values which are 'direct, practical, concerned with behaviour and experience rather than words and images, and as such are in conflict with the verbal methods and values of traditional education'.[3]

Raymond Williams shows how the problem of communication in a society which is on the whole literate but deeply divided educationally and socially, is met by the rise of stereotyped formulas. These are the patterns used by the media (newspapers, magazines and radio) and considered by Williams, who shows that the assumptions and conventions about the content and presentation of material to the two sections of society can become rigidly entrenched and hence resistant to change. So the masses are fed on crime, sex, sport, personalities, entertainment and pictorial presentations, whilst 'the minority' are given traditional politics, traditional arts, and briefings on popular trends. It is then a matter for argument, Williams says, 'whether "the masses" and "the minority" are inevitably social facts, or whether they are communication models which in part create and reinforce the situation they apparently describe'.[4]

[1] *ibid.*, p. 187.
[2] *ibid.*, p. 191.
[3] *ibid.* See also Richard Hoggart, *The Uses of Literacy*, Penguin, 1958.
[4] Raymond Williams, *Communications*, Chatto, 1966, p. 96.

We can now look at findings regarding the more specific effects of one of the mass media which has been studied more thoroughly. This is television, and we shall present some of the conclusions regarding its effects on children, young people, the family and political behaviour. Among the earliest empirical studies concerned with the first aspect were those by Hilde Himmelweit and her team. As concerns displacement effects, i.e. time taken up by viewing, the chief conclusions were that contrary to popular belief children did not watch programmes indiscriminately; the single most important determinant of the amount of viewing done by the child was his intelligence, whilst the social level of the home did not affect this aspect very much. Secondary influencing factors were the child's personality (and how full and active a life he led before television was introduced), as well as parental example.[1] Regarding the effects of programme content, results suggested that a large number of programmes containing violence are likely to make a cumulative impact, particularly on younger children.[2] On the whole, however, Himmelweit maintains that television is 'not as black as it is painted, but neither is it the great harbinger of culture and enlightenment', although children did acquire certain values and an outlook on life consistent with the contents of television programmes.[3] A more general survey by Mark Abrams suggests that the long-term combined effect of television viewing and the increased consumption of the printed mass media, is one of broadening the outlook of the younger generation; making them aware not only of their family circle, neighbourhood and workplace, but also of the wider community and other societies.[4]

[1] H. T. Himmelweit *et al.*, *Television and the Child*, O.U.P., 1958, pp. 11–14.

[2] See Himmelweit quoted in J. D. Halloran, *The Effects of Mass Communication*, Leicester U.P., 1964, p. 34.

[3] Himmelweit, *op. cit.*, p. 40, and Halloran, *op. cit.*, p. 14.

[4] Mark Abrams, *The Newspaper Reading Public of Tomorrow*, Odhams, 1964.

As far as family life is concerned, W. A. Belson found that his enquiry did not throw up any evidence which might suggest that television produces radical changes. Thus it slightly reduces home-centred and joint activity, but it also brings the family together. There may in some cases be more substantial reductions in the collective frequency and the range of sociable activities, but after about five years there is a tendency for these to return to the pre-television level.[1] Belson stresses at the same time the importance of other factors and states: 'It is clear that the effects of television on family life and on sociability are highly sensitive to local and seasonal factors. They depend, among other things, upon the viewer's cultural and family backgrounds, and upon the area in which he lives'.[2]

Considering the effects of television on political attitudes in a study at the time of the 1959 general election, Trenaman came to the conclusion that there were certain protective devices at work during election campaigns which screened off electors and at least temporarily suppressed any direct effects, particularly once electors recognized the campaign as propaganda aimed at them. On the whole, group pressures reduced the effects of propaganda and an element of free choice was also at work.[3] A PEP report holds that some views, particularly about politics, religion and social class, are rather resistant to change; but in relation to many new issues, where public attitudes are not yet formed or in cases where people either have conflicting opinions or do not feel strongly about an issue, there is a greater susceptibility to persuasion by the mass media. The report argues that this is bound to have an

[1] W. A. Belson, *Television and the Family*, Audience Research Dept, BBC, 1959, p. 131.

[2] *ibid.*, p. 127.

[3] J. Trenaman and Denis McQuail, *Television and the Political Image*, Methuen, 1961, pp. 202–4.

effect on civic goals and hence on society as a whole.[1] The potency of television is, according to J. D. Halloran, evident in another sense, that is in the influence it brings to bear on the other mass media: 'The radio, cinema, theatre, and magazine are being compelled to change'.[2]

Finally, sociologists have considered the process of attitude formation and change as affected by mass communication. Bryan Wilson, whilst noting that these processes are not yet capable of being accurately measured because of their subtle and gradual nature, suggests that the media are altering our attitudes as concerns crime. They promote values which 'stand in stark contrast to the values entrenched in our existing social institutions—the family, the work-place, the school, the law courts, the church—and in our social relation-ships'. He claims that the new values are more tolerant of deviant behaviour, and that this results in the mass media 'promoting the erosion of traditional social values and . . . creating confusion, particularly among young people, about standards of behaviour'.[3] Halloran points out that Wilson does not produce sociological evidence to substantiate this indictment of the mass media. But although Halloran's review of research in the area points to a view that 'the mass media are not as powerful as personal and direct experience in changing attitudes', he agrees that 'their potential cannot be played down'.[4] He proposed, therefore, that research be undertaken to establish more accurately the role of the media as socializing agents and their relationship to other means of social control, and insists on the need to adopt for the purposes

[1] *Citizenship and Television*, a PEP report written by J. G. Blumler and John Madge, 1965, esp. pp. 7, 46, 47.

[2] Halloran, *op. cit.*, p. 16.

[3] *ibid.*, p. 27 (Halloran quotes from Wilson's article in *Criminal Law Review*).

[4] J. D. Halloran, *Attitude Formation and Change*, Leicester U.P., 1967, p. 88.

of such research an inclusive sociological model. Halloran emphasises the necessity of setting communications research in the wider social context in view of the fact that 'neither the communicator nor the recipient operate in isolation', and further stresses that this is 'a problem area which involves interrelationships between the various components in a social structure'.[1]

DEVIANCE

Despite much research in this area there is a great deal of uncertainty about the incidence of crime and delinquency in modern society as compared with earlier periods. While Leon Radzinowicz sees no sign of a turn in the increasing tide of criminal behaviour of the mid-twentieth century,[2] Barbara Wootton advises caution in the interpretation of crime statistics and maintains that it is now generally recognized that such evidence is unreliable for making long-term comparisons.[3] Again, while there is some evidence to confirm that high-delinquency areas are to be found in the big cities and ports rather than in rural areas,[4] it has been pointed out by Leslie Wilkins that 'areas which have had a bad reputation among those who may be expected to know do not always turn out to be high-delinquency areas when rigorous data are obtained'.[5]

On the other hand there is a good deal of agreement

---

[1] *ibid.*, p. 119; and see Halloran, *The Effects of Mass Communication*, *op. cit.*, pp. 28, 29.

[2] Leon Radzinowicz, *Ideology and Crime*, Heinemann, 1966, p. 61.

[3] Barbara Wootton, *Social Science and Social Pathology*, Allen & Unwin, 1959, p. 24.

[4] Max Grunhut, *Juvenile Offenders before the Courts*, Clarendon Press, Oxford, 1956, p. 120.

[5] Leslie Wilkins, *Social Deviance*, Tavistock, 1964, p. 210.

regarding sociological explanations of deviance in our society. Many writers stress the changes in the social structure which modern industrial conditions have wrought, and either explicitly or implicitly invoke this as the basic reason for the increase in most criminal behaviour in contemporary society. We summarize below the main points that arise from this view. (1) Lack of cohesion and adequate means of social control due to the impersonalization of social relationships in the highly industrialized city are reflected in weakening kinship ties and community bonds, and lead to a breakdown in culture and the normative system and to a condition of *anomie*.[1] (2) Impersonal social relations resulting in the victim of the crime receding into anonymity, and greater affluence which means more opportunity to commit crime, are factors which encourage criminal behaviour.[2] (3) Thwarted aspirations in some sections of the population, for whom avenues of social mobility are generally closed despite the stress put in contemporary society on achievement-orientation, lead to discontent, rejection of both working-class and middle-class values, and so to rebelliousness, particularly in teenage groups, ending up in deviance.[3]

Leaving aside these general views expressed regarding crime, there are studies which deal with particular types of deviant behaviour. Thus Michael Schofield's research findings showed clearly that there were important differences between homosexuals and paedophiliacs, probably in their aetiologies and certainly in the social consequences involved. 'One of the most striking facts to emerge', Schofield states, 'was that a

[1] See, e.g., Terence Morris, 'The Sociology of Crime', *New Society*, 29 April 1965. It is interesting to note that Morris poses a question to sociologists who have produced reassuring studies showing that the family as an institution is not in decline (see above, p. 109).

[2] *ibid.*, and Radzinowicz, *op. cit.*

[3] B. Wilson, *op. cit*; T. R. Fyvel, *The Insecure Offenders*, Chatto, 1961, p. 203ff; P. Willmott, *Adolescent Boys of East London*, *op. cit.*, pp. 167–8.

homosexual who is sexually attracted to adult men is hardly ever a danger to children, and paedophiliacs are only very rarely interested in sexual activities with adult males. Indeed over a quarter of the men in prison for offences with young boys had also sexually assaulted young girls'.[1] Another study which distinguishes between different types of deviance is that which was carried out by Harriet Wilson. She compared delinquency resulting from the neglect of children by parents who do not instil moral values in them, with delinquency arising from a home where moral standards are upheld. The acts of delinquency differ, therefore, in that in the former the child is ignorant of the kind of behaviour required of him, whilst in the latter he is aware of required standards but deviates despite this. She concludes that 'If this is true it follows that future delinquency research must learn to differentiate between such different activities as "neglect-delinquency", "environmental delinquescent behaviour", "guilt-delinquency" and so on. It may then be possible to find out which type of delinquency is most frequently linked with recidivism; which type of delinquency is most likely to develop into adult criminality, and possibly also into which type of adult criminality'.[2]

We shall now turn our attention to some of the results regarding juvenile delinquency. Basing himself on a piece of operational research, carried out in the context of a new type of boys' club, Mays stresses that for many delinquent boys the environmental and social factors of their sub-cultural background can be shown to cause delinquent infection. According to Mays his findings serve 'to underline the great social importance of family life and relationships in determining the way in which a child copes with the delinquent

---

[1] Michael Schofield, 'Child Molesters', *New Society*, 14 Oct. 1965, p. 11, and his *The Sociological Aspects of Homosexuality*, *op. cit.*

[2] Harriet Wilson, *op. cit.*, p. 147.

associations of an admittedly criminogenic environment'.[1]
Mays points to the inadequacies of the environment due to the
existing sub-culture, which is to be overcome by group-work
agencies filling in the gaps and by introducing the culture of
the wider society into these 'substandard neighbourhoods'.[2]
A somewhat different slant is given to the problem of juvenile
delinquency by David Downes, who is doubtful about the
very use of the concept of delinquent sub-culture. He maintains that the concept 'is not wholly satisfactory since "sub-
culture" is too readily applied as a blanket term to any set of
sub-group norms, values and beliefs that deviate from an
ideal-type dominant middle-class normative system'.[3] Taking
into account post-war work on delinquency and his own
research in two inner London boroughs, he attempts to
modify the sub-cultural theory. He argues that the working-
class boy starts out in a delinquency-prone rather than in a
conformity-promoting life situation. This observation in itself
is not very different from that made by Mays. But Downes
stresses that in research the basic assumption is all-important.
A conformity-promoting view leads the researcher to look for
the factors which divert the boy from conformity to deviance,
e.g. broken homes. The delinquency-prone premise would
regard such factors as aggravating rather than intervening,
and research would, therefore, have to be directed towards
variables which keep the working-class boy *from* delinquency, e.g. 'college-boy' performance at school.[4] In sum
Downes lays greater stress on prevention than cure and
attempts to direct research along such lines.

A number of studies have concentrated attention on offenders who have been dealt with by the law and who are found

[1] J. B. Mays, *On the Threshold of Delinquency*, Liverpool U.P., 1959,
p. 210. See also Mays, *Crime and the Social Structure*, Faber, 1963.
[2] *ibid.*, pp. ix, 211.
[3] D. M. Downes, *The Delinquent Solution*, Routledge, 1966, p. 225.
[4] *ibid.*, pp. 259, 260.

in institutions such as prisons or Borstals. In a study of this nature Alan Little found, after the application of tests, that the 'cultural' hypothesis was correct. According to this hypothesis there is in a penal institution an anti-staff, anti-system, and anti-institution culture.[1] In the Borstal he investigated he found that 'the popular inmate tends to have a more unfavourable attitude to the staff and system than the unpopular'.[2] One of the results of Gordon Westwood's study of the male homosexual shows that there was an 'agreement with the many theories which suggest that homosexual tendencies develop in children from unsatisfactory homes, but it does not account for 30 per cent of contacts who came from apparently undisturbed backgrounds'.[3] In G. E. Levens' study of 'white-collar criminals' the overall conclusion is that whilst prison sentence does result in a loss of social and occupational status, it does not on the whole bring about a loss of middle-class status.[4] The main conclusion reached by Terence and Pauline Morris in their detailed study of Pentonville prison is that the negative effects of prison life on offenders are caused in the main by the adverse environment. The latter includes the existing physical conditions and the attitudes of prison staff and the public, in that these environmental factors are conducive to merely controlling the prisoner rather than attempting to improve him.[5]

As Terence Morris concludes elsewhere, 'if sociological research into the prison community has done nothing else, it has questioned certain long-held assumptions about the role of the prison and has thrown into relief once more the question "what is prison for?"' But whilst Morris can see that the prison may often be an irrelevant interlude in a

[1] Little, *op. cit.*, p. 130.
[2] *ibid.*, p. 195.
[3] Westwood, *op. cit.*, p. 192.
[4] Levens, *op. cit.*, p. 135.
[5] Terence and Pauline Morris, *op. cit.*

career of crime, he also states that there appear to be few realistic alternatives. The true function of the prison may, therefore, be no more than symbolic, 'a statement that, even if penal treatments neither reform nor deter, at least society has expressed its disapproval of crime'.[1] Finally, the question of rehabilitation after prison sentence has been considered by some writers. If Levens has been able to show, as we have seen above, that 'white-collar criminals' have few problems of reintegration in society, this may have been because this group, as John Spencer says, is hardly regarded as criminal, and possibly also because they display a high degree of social mobility.[2] On the other hand, many difficulties are encountered in finding employment for other ex-prisoners, the crucial problem both for prison and after-care being, according to J. P. Martin, 'how to break down the division between prison and society'.[3]

We can make the modest claim for the above studies that they help to clarify the effects of the special institutions and of society at large on the lives of offenders.

MINORITY GROUPS AND RACE RELATIONS

With regard to differentiation in society along racial and ethnic lines and the problem of group relations that such differentiation creates, the general conclusions reached by most studies point to various degrees of integration being achieved. This conclusion is hardly exciting in itself but there

[1] Terence Morris, 'The Sociology of Prison', in T. Grygier *et al.* (eds.), *Criminology in Transition: Essays in Honour of Hermann Mannheim*, Tavistock, 1965, p. 83.
[2] John C. Spencer, 'White-collar Crime', *ibid.*, p. 233ff.
[3] J. P. Martin, 'After-Care in Transition', *ibid.*, p. 107. See also his 'Employing Ex-Prisoners', *New Society*, 3 Oct. 1963, pp. 18, 19, and his *Offenders as Employees*, Macmillan, 1962.

is a good deal of interest in the quantitative results, i.e. the extent to which integration is achieved in different spheres. In the case of the West Indians, for instance, Sheila Patterson says: 'A fair degree of migrant accommodation in work, somewhat less in housing and the modest beginnings of migrant acclimatization and local acquiescence in casual and formal social contacts—this, then, was the general position in Brixton in mid-1959'.[1] The same tendency towards accommodation is shown in the studies relating to Indian immigrants.[2] In the case of the Jews, too, the accommodation consists in the fine balance which this minority achieves by acculturating to the larger society but not allowing itself to be completely assimilated. Thus, the Jews in Leeds were not being structurally absorbed into the wider society but they did succumb to the process of acculturation by giving up a good deal of their own cultural distinctiveness and by adopting the external cultural aspects of the wider society.[3] As far as the Irish immigrants are concerned, their adjustment to life in Britain, according to J. A. Jackson, must be seen in the light of 'the changing relationships between peoples closely linked by traditional association and yet sharply divided by historical circumstances'.[4] The Irish immigrant is not much of a stranger in Britain, yet his former home is so near that he does not relinquish his (real or sentimental) links with it and this maintains his Irish identity. The Irish immigrant has done more, however, than just accommodate to his new life in Britain. Jackson maintains that 'over the past two hundred years it has been the immigrant from Ireland to Britain who

---

[1] S. Patterson, *op. cit.*, p. 396.

[2] See, e.g., Rashmi Desai, *Indian Immigrants in Britain*, o.u.p., 1963, p. 145, and G. S. Aurora, 'Indian Workers in England: a Sociological and Historical Survey', unpbl. m.sc. thesis, Univ. of London, 1960, p. 244.

[3] E. Krausz, *op. cit.*, pp. 135-7.

[4] Jackson, *op. cit.*, p. 161.

has provided a bond and sustained a tenuous link between the Irish and the rest of Britain'.

It is important to note that the adjustment immigrants make is influenced not only by conditions in Britain but also by more basic factors such as their home (native) backgrounds and their educational, occupational and general status. As far as the latter factors are concerned, C. E. Fiscian concludes in the case of West Indians in London that 'the expression of hostile attitudes towards the English is higher in the section with lower status, with a low level of education, and among whom the incidence of unemployment is high. . . .'[1] In a more general vein, in connection with Indian students in Britain, A. K. Singh says that 'coming to Britain was not an isolated event, a closed and cut off period. . . . It was fitted into and completed the pattern of their lives. Their experiences in this country were influenced by their conditions back at home and their future aspirations'.[2] On the whole, there appears to be not enough knowledge regarding either the background factors or the actual scene of adjustment. And Ruth Glass concludes that 'the keynote in the situation of the coloured minority in Britain is not inflexible prejudice, harsh segregation and discrimination; it is muddle, confusion and insecurity. And it is both a cause and a symptom of this muddle—of the confusion of the white and the consequent confusion of the coloured—that so little is known about the newcomer'.[3] A worthwhile beginning has nevertheless been made, and the studies mentioned above as well as the discussion which follows testify to this.

An important area considered in relation to all minority groups has been that of the process of adjustment, in particu-

[1] C. E. Fiscian, 'Minority Group Prejudice', unpbl. ph.d. thesis, Univ. of London, 1960, p. 400.
[2] A. K. Singh, 'Indian Students in Britain', unpbl. ph.d. thesis, Univ. of London, 1961, p. 124.
[3] Ruth Glass, *Newcomers, op. cit.*, p. 212.

lar the kind of adjustment termed 'assimilation'.[1] The question is whether this is a one-way or a two-way process. Is there adjustment on behalf of both immigrants and hosts, or is it only the former who have to adjust? S. F. Collins has pointed out that conflicts between coloured groups and the white population are lessened where the latter are more dispersed.[2] Whilst saying that this observation may be correct, Michael Banton voiced disagreement with the implication that Collins' statement might contain, i.e. 'the implication that assimilation is facilitated by dispersal'.[3] Banton regarded this view as being 'in line with the conception of assimilation as a one-way process requiring no modifications from the majority group, but only good behaviour on the part of the immigrants'. On the basis of his study of coloured immigrants in East London, he contends that 'the principal obstacle to assimilation is the attitude of English people towards coloured persons'. Assimilation is the result, therefore, of a two-way process of adjustment. Vakis Nearchou, who looked at the Cypriot community in London, disagrees with this standpoint. He maintains that in the case of the Cypriots there is a one-way process of assimilation. The Cypriots are, according to him, moving through a one-way process of acculturation, towards complete assimilation. In the conflict of cultures there are no reciprocal adjustments; the English culture triumphs for it is the more suited for the country.[4] Maurice Freedman's conclusions regarding the Jewish minority, however, seem to support Banton's arguments. Assimilation for the Jews may mean different things according to which seg-

[1] See above, pp. 52–7, for a discussion of concepts and terms including 'assimilation'.

[2] S. F. Collins, *Coloured Minorities in Britain*, Lutterworth, 1957.

[3] Michael Banton, *The Coloured Quarter*, Cape, 1955, p. 235.

[4] Vakis Nearchou, 'The Assimilation of the Cypriot Community in London', unpbl. M.A. thesis, Univ. of Nottingham, 1960, pp. 194, 197–9, 237–8.

ments of the minority one considers. Similarly there are varying criteria of assimilation—formal, social, and so on. Again, he stresses that acculturation and assimilation are linked and help to determine together the place that the minority finds for itself in the wider society. But for the determination of this place much depends also on how the non-Jews view the stance that the Jews adopt and what acceptances and resistances the former evince. Thus he says: 'The sense of being both British and a Jew, which is clearly the aim of many—witness the fervent identification with the symbols of both—measures the degree to which Jews have assimilated only if we know how far the world of non-Jews accepts the combination'.[1] In this sense, therefore, assimilation must be regarded as a two-way process of adjustment.

The problem arises, however, whether the very terms of 'assimilation' and 'acculturation' can be usefully applied to different types of minority.[2] In a recent study of suburban Jews in London the present writer points out in fact that, for example, the conceptual framework of conflict–accommodation–assimilation is not suitable for the study of that minority group.[3] A. H. Richmond, who reviewed the earlier studies of race relations in Britain, concludes nonetheless that 'Despite some terminological confusion . . . all investigations appear to agree that the Jewish, Moslem and Chinese immigrants, who have adapted themselves to conditions in Britain but not, in the main, attempted complete assimilation as individuals, have made the most successful adjustment. African and West Indian Negroes, whose Christian education

---

[1] Maurice Freedman, *A Minority in Britain*, Vallentine Mitchell, 1955, pp. 203, 227, 239ff.

[2] See above, p. 55.

[3] E. Krausz, 'A Sociological Field Study of Jewish Suburban Life in Edgware 1962–3, with Special Reference to Minority Identification', unpbl. PH.D. thesis, Univ. of London, 1965, p. 202ff.

has given them expectations of life in Britain that are not in practice realizable, are much more exposed to conflict and are less well adjusted'.[1]

The existence of a conflict situation has also been stressed in a recent study of race relations in Birmingham. John Rex and Robert Moore see the conflicts and the realistic adjustments leading to truce situations as taking place within a special kind of social system. This is the 'zone of transition' of the large industrial city, where there is a constant struggle for housing and where tension management usually achieves some kind of reconciliation between the various opposing interests. The authors stress that this kind of situation does not warrant the use of the host–immigrant framework, and that the 'balance of power' situation to which their study draws attention is easily confused with situations of 'accommodation' or 'pluralistic integration'. Rex and Moore argue that the results of their study show that the race relations situation in Birmingham, and quite likely in most Western industrial cities, must be seen in the wider context of the sociology of the city. They state that 'the particular aspects of race relations with which we have been concerned are explicable only in terms of the sociology of the city' and the central point to this is 'that there is a class struggle over the use of houses and that this struggle is the central process of the city as a social unit'.[2] This struggle, however, does not only concern coloured immigrant groups, for in addition to these there were the Irish and other depressed groups, and what developed was a complex system of power relations. Seen as a whole, the 'zone of transition' is not so much an exclusively immigrant 'ghetto' as a special area of the city

[1] Anthony H. Richmond, 'Britain', in *Research on Racial Relations*, UNESCO, 1966, p. 208.
[2] J. Rex and R. Moore, *Race, Community and Conflict*, O.U.P., 1967, pp. 272–3, and see mainly the introduction and ch. 12.

with peculiar problems of its own which includes that of the coloured immigrant in his urban setting.[1]

Michael Banton similarly points to the fact that the host–immigrant perspective is no longer adequate to the study of the British scene and that empirical evidence may suggest a shift from integrationist theories to conflict theories, from consensus to dissensus.[2] Reviewing the position of race relations in Britain, Banton emphasizes some of the points stressed by Rex and Moore, and these together with his predictions as to the possible future situation are expressed in his main conclusion: 'The sanctions of the homogeneous society, of the small community based upon personal acquaintance, are not effective in industrial societies. If the second generation of immigrant children are not enabled to compete fairly with their age-mates for work and housing they may prove a rebellious and expensive minority. In an industrial society the costs of disaffection are heavy, whether it be on a basis of class, religion, region, or race, but if it be race there is the added complication that intergroup friction has international significance'.[3]

The output of literature and reports of research in the area of minorities, and particularly race relations, has been enormous in recent years.[4] We have tried to give above only the main trends in research and some of the important results but have inevitably left out a good deal of interesting, but rather more specialized, material.[5]

[1] *ibid.*
[2] Michael Banton, *Race Relations*, Tavistock, 1967, pp. 62–8.
[3] *ibid.*, p. 393.
[4] Sivanandan lists some 600 publications since 1950 in the field of race relations. He estimates that the output has increased fourfold in the last two years. See A. Sivanandan, *Coloured Immigrants in Britain: a Select Bibliography*, Institute of Race Relations, Oct. 1967.
[5] See, e.g., Nicholas Deakin (ed.), *Colour and the British Electorate*, Pall Mall, 1965.

RELIGION

Looking for the results of the studies dealing with the sociology of religion, we find that the integrative aspects of religion
have mainly been stressed. John Highet, for instance, points
out how earlier in this century in Scotland the local church,
even in the cities, was the focal point of many activities in
addition to the purely religious activities.[1] The study by
Conor Ward in Liverpool highlights the parish as providing
closely knit social units for many within the limited geographical areas. And he points out that 'emphasis on the importance
of the parish unit had brought about a widespread acceptance
of an ideal of parochial loyalty'.[2]

The integrative effects of religion within fissionary or
partly segregated groups also come to the fore in a number of
studies. Whilst on the face of it the very existence of such
groups suggests divisiveness when society is taken as a whole,
the fact is that religion usually acts in such groups as a factor
of social control. It irons out certain problems for the members
of the groups. Thus one can see that in certain circumstances
internal group integration ensures the necessary inter-group
adjustments for society as a whole. According to Bryan
Wilson, sects act as small 'deviant' reference groups which
enable the individual to gain more favourable status and
prestige than are available in the wider society. The sect
provides 'the reassurance of a stable, affective society. . . .
Its ideological orientation and its group cohesion provide a
context of emotional security'.[3] In the case of minority groups,
too, religion has worked as a cohesive force. The present
writer has pointed out that among Jews membership of the
synagogue, and even just occasional worship and activity in
it, provides a major avenue of identification with Judaism

[1] John Highet, *The Churches in Scotland Today*, *op. cit.*, p. 70.
[2] *op. cit.*, p. 117.
[3] Bryan Wilson, *op. cit.*, p. 354.

and the Jewish minority.[1] Within the Christian fold membership of churches or sects specifically linked with particular
minority groups is an important factor in the identification of
the individual with his in-group. Poles in Britain belong to
separate Polish Roman Catholic parishes.[2] The Irish, on the
other hand, re-established Catholicism in Britain, and 'the
Roman Catholic Church has played an important part in
preserving Irish interests among the immigrants'.[3] It has also
been pointed out that West Indians have brought with them
special Pentecostal sects to which they belong and which
provide them, in the strange setting, with 'a buffer against
the society at large'.[4]

Concerning the kinds of organization, doctrinal alignments
and relations to secular institutions, David Martin points out
that for Christians in Britain there are numerous options
which represent different combinations and developments
produced by a long period of Christian germination and
general historical events. 'Sociologists have developed a
shorthand for reducing the infinite variety of these options to
three basic "types" which between them include an enormous
range of possibilities'.[5] The three models are 'church',
'denomination' and 'sect'. Martin's analysis points up the
predominant characteristics exhibited by these type-con-
structs. The 'church' claims social inclusiveness, identifies
with the State, has a sacred hierarchy and insists on a com-

[1] Ernest Krausz, 'A Sociological Field Study of Jewish Suburban Life
in Edgware 1962-3, with Special Reference to Minority Identification',
unpbl. PH.D. thesis, Univ. of London, 1965, p. 192.

[2] Zubrzycki, *op. cit.*, ch. 9, and Sheila Patterson, 'Polish London' in
London, Centre for Urban Studies, p. 326ff.

[3] See Jackson, *The Irish in Britain, op. cit.*, ch. 7; also Jackson in *London*,
op. cit., p. 306.

[4] M. Calley, 'West Indian Churches in England', *New Society*, 6 Aug.
1964, p. 18.

[5] David Martin, *A Sociology of English Religion*, Heinemann, 1967, p.
78.

prehensive dogmatic scheme with the accent on past events. The denomination is usually not a social majority, explicitly separates itself from the State but does not reject the wider society, uses a pragmatic division of authority roles and has a system of psychological dynamics with emphasis on present conversion. The 'sect' is typically a small exclusive dispossessed minority, which radically rejects society and its institutions, has a tendency to reject functionaries and emphasizes comprehensive indoctrination and the future. Martin recognizes that these are gross simplifications and regards the 'ideal type' constructs as useful heuristic tools rather than representing substantive descriptions.[1]

Bryan Wilson proposes an even more rigid attitude to such typologies. He says, for instance, that 'It is not difficult to show that the application of type constructs—namely that all sects are more or less similar in organization, ideology, social composition, communal character and circumstances of origin—has very little warrant'.[2] He shows that the older sects associated mainly with rural communities exhibit little *religious* organization as such, being subsumed in the community structure and using religious sanctions mainly as 'boundary-maintaining devices'. On the other hand, sects not backed up by strong community allegiance necessarily develop and rely on specially devised organizational structures. 'But even here', he says, 'a distinction can be made between movements which place more reliance on common doctrinal commitment and those which rely more on an authority structure to determine the arrangements of association'.[3] Roland Robertson, a contributor to one of Wilson's volumes, shows that considering developments in the Salvation Army it would be superficial to accept the general view of change in religious movement being a transition from a position of

[1] *ibid.*, pp. 78, 79n., 80.
[2] B. R. Wilson (ed.), *Patterns of Sectarianism*, Heinemann, 1967, p. 3.
[3] *ibid.*, p. 13.

separateness from secular society to one of accommodation with it, that is simply a change from sect to denomination.[1]

Despite the above points, Wilson's own studies and those of some of his co-authors point to many similarities—for instance, between different sects. One such recurrent tendency is that 'in the last analysis sectarian commitment is always voluntary, whatever operates to elicit it'. Another common characteristic is that 'sects display a distinctive and deviant response to the world'. Furthermore, these similar trends were observable also in other social movements which have common elements with sects. It should also be noted that Wilson does use certain models, or sub-types if related to the wider models, in his presentation of a collection of papers. These are: conversionist sects, e.g. the Salvation Army; introversionist sects, e.g. the Quakers; and non-sectarian movements, e.g. humanist societies.[2]

Turning to the wider scene a general trend towards secularization is pointed to by sociologists,[3] but they also warn against underestimating the influence of religion, even if the latter appears to be on the decline. John Highet, referring to the process of secularization, maintains that 'It would be an oversimplification. . . . to invoke this change as evidence of a lack of "church-mindedness" in contemporary Scotland'. He contends that certain changes in modern society were bound to affect the Church together with other social institutions, however religiously minded the population, but that these changes need not necessarily have produced a considerable deterioration in religious attitudes.[4] Bryan Wilson also points out that 'The ways in which men express their

[1] Roland Robertson, 'The Salvation Army—the Persistence of Sectarianism', *ibid.*, p. 49.

[2] *ibid.*

[3] See, e.g., Alasdair MacIntyre, *Secularization and Moral Change*, O.U.P., 1967.

[4] John Highet, *op. cit.*, p. 71.

"religiosity" may be changing, and church attendance and ritual may be felt by some quite religiously disposed people to be outworn patterns unadapted to the modern world'. In view of this he argues that statistics about religion must be carefully interpreted, particularly when using them to show comparative trends in religiousness. Yet he maintains that 'the statistics do provide some evidence of significant religious change. They are some sort of index of secularization, taking that word at its common sense value'.[1] As far as trends in secularization are concerned, Wilson thinks that the assessment must be made not only in terms of ideological developments but also of institutional persistence. He points to the fact that churches exist as structures, operated by a professional service, factors which ensure their continuance—'even if they lose social importance . . . they are unlikely to disappear'.[2] In his final conclusion he doubts whether secular society could function without the institution of religion. 'The secular society of the present, in which religious thinking, practices and institutions, have but a small part, is none the less the inheritor of values, dispositions and orientations from the religious past. The completely secularized society has not yet existed. Whether indeed our own type of society will effectively maintain public order, without institutional coercion, once the still persisting influence of past religion wanes even further, remains to be seen'.[3]

David Martin also maintains that religion exhibits a good deal of strength. This can be seen mainly in the steadying influence it exerts in the conditions of a rapidly changing contemporary society. Martin says that 'there is plenty of evidence that for many people the church acts as the still point in a turning world'. It becomes an important point of

[1] Wilson, *op. cit.*, p. 2.
[2] *ibid.*, p. 54.
[3] *ibid.*, p. 233.

reference but one lagging behind the points of change. This produces a certain amount of confusion which induces people to opt out of full involvement and to go merely for some of the symbolic aspects. In certain milieux, however, religion is on the losing side. Martin can see for instance that 'Mobility at a higher level . . . can even erode church attachments'.[1] The overall view, based on the conclusions of writers mentioned, is, however, that religion in Britain is far from a completely spent force.

So far as the concept of secularization is concerned, some sociologists have accepted a workable or commonsense meaning, amongst them Bryan Wilson. David Martin on the other hand has argued in favour of eliminating the use of this term, which according to him is misleading and which he regards as a barrier to progress in the sociology of religion.[2] The reason why he puts forward this view is that the term cannot serve as a scientific concept because it is too closely bound up with distortions resulting from its use as a tool of counter-religious ideologies.

Finally, a brief review of the sociology of religion in England by J. A. Banks brings out one interesting point. Most of the research has had as its main concern the organizational aspects of religious groups and their relations to the wider society. At the same time little attention has so far been given to the analysis of religious teachings and to a comparison of the belief systems of science, magic and religion.[3]

[1] David Martin, *A Sociology of English Religion*, *op. cit.*, pp. 109, 111. See also the point of view put forward by Brennan and his colleagues that it is not so much a loss of belief by its membership as the inability of the church to keep pace with rapid social change that is causing its decline (T. Brennan *et al.*, *Social Change in South-west Wales*, Watts, 1954).

[2] Martin, 'Towards Eliminating the Concept of Secularization', in Julius Gould (ed.), *Penguin Survey of the Social Sciences*, Penguin, 1965, p. 169ff.

[3] J. A. Banks, 'The Sociology of Religion in England', in Joan Brothers (ed.), *Readings in the Sociology of Religion*, Pergamon, 1967, p. 68.

WORK AND LEISURE

A number of sociologists have drawn attention to the over-concentration of British research on the purely industrial aspects of work. This strong emphasis is explicable in terms of the major changes that industrialization wrought for most people, particularly where their work takes place in the industrial sector of the economy. Nonetheless, J. A. Banks maintains that 'a full sociology of work would extend the frontiers of empirical knowledge into the vocational activities of lawyers, of doctors, of clergymen, of politicians, of police-men, of entertainers, of farmers, as well as of industrial managers and their employers'.[1] As we shall see below, a number of studies dealing with occupations outside the purely industrial setting have been carried out, but it is still true to say with Stephen Cotgrove that the study of occupations, and particularly the influence that a particular occupation has on other areas of life such as the family and leisure activities, has been largely ignored.[2] We shall return to this somewhat neglected area, but first an account will be given of some of the important findings of industrial sociology.[3]

The results of some of the studies in this field are particularly interesting since they concern the workers' attitudes to industrial change. One of the early studies by the Liverpool University team of researchers showed that in the complexity of factors influencing attitudes to such change, earnings, job status and the altered social life of the workers were of

[1] J. A. Banks, 'The Sociology of Work', in T. R. Fyvel (ed.), *The Frontiers of Sociology*, Cohen & West, 1964, p. 24. It should be noted that since Banks' writing at least two of the occupations he mentions have been investigated: see M. Banton, *The Policeman and the Community*, Tavistock, 1964; and Brian Abel-Smith and R. Stevens, *Lawyers and the Courts*, Heinemann, 1967.

[2] S. Cotgrove, *The Science of Society*, Allen & Unwin, 1967, p. 143.

[3] For a detailed but fairly concise account of this area see S. R. Parker *et al.*, *The Sociology of Industry*, Allen & Unwin, 1967.

particular importance.[1] In a follow-up study, Olive Banks came to the conclusion that 'There is no evidence of any widespread hostility to technical change as such' and that 'It would appear that employees are more adaptable than is sometimes supposed, and can adjust to the need for job transfers without lasting resentment'.[2] She did qualify her findings, however, by saying that the men who formed the groups placed under scrutiny were mostly 'with long service in an industry which is noted for good management–union relationships, and in a firm with a history of successful assimilation of a number of periods of technical change'. Although J. A. Banks concentrated on the aspect of workers' 'participation' in industry, his results are relevant to the more general study of the relationship between workers' attitudes and technical change. He says that, considering his findings, 'it is, for example, now possible to assert that all other things being equal, the more a technical change results in smaller working teams and a general upgrading of skill, the greater the extent of participation on the part of the work force which remains. The more it results in larger teams and a downgrading of skills, the smaller the participation'. J. A. Banks also concludes that the influences of the traditions of the occupation or of the trade union connected with the occupation are of far less importance in determining workers' attitudes to participation than the actual jobs they have.[3]

A recurring theme found in the results of researches about worker/management behaviour is that this must be understood in the light of the relationship between the internal factors of the factory, workshop or firm and the external factors of the economy, technology and social structure. Joan Woodward has stressed the importance of economic and

[1] W. H. Scott *et al.*, *op. cit.*, ch. 5.
[2] O. Banks, *The Attitudes of Steel Workers to Technical Change, op. cit.*, pp. 132–3.
[3] J. A. Banks, *Industrial Participation, op. cit.*, p. 134.

technological factors in the examination of behaviour in the workshop.[1] Following Woodward's argument that 'economic circumstances, technology and administration are not independent but inter-dependent variables', J. D. Mather concludes that the variation in foremen's roles from factory to factory 'can be attributed to a set of factors which are external to a foreman's immediate situation in that they are determined by forces largely outside the control of the foreman, his managers, or any other single authority'.[2] As a result of interviews with shop stewards and observation in an electrical engineering firm, Anne Bird concludes that 'economic and technological variables proved important in explaining the occurrence of certain patterns of dispute in the workshop'.[3] Finally, T. Lupton's work shows that certain combinations or clusters of 'external' and 'internal' factors determine the particular kind of worker behaviour in relation to control over output and earnings found in different factories. He lists the external factors as: market (stability and size), competition, scale of industry, location of industry, trade unions, cost ratio and products; and the internal factors as: method of wage payment, productive system, sex of workers, workshop social structure and management/worker relationship.[4] His analysis of workshop behaviour also led Lupton to refute earlier notions about 'restriction of output'. In previous studies it was thought that such restrictions were due to the incompatibility of management's logic of efficiency and workers' 'groupishness', the latter resulting in irrational reactions of custom and

[1] Joan Woodward, 'Management and Technology', HMSO, 1959, p. 18. See also *Industrial Organization: Theory and Practice*, O.U.P., 1965.

[2] J. D. Mather, 'A Comparative Sociological Study of Foremen in Two Engineering Factories in North-west England', unpbl. M.A.Econ. thesis, Univ. of Manchester, 1959, pp. 217, 227.

[3] Anne D. Bird, 'A Sociological Analysis of Management/Worker Conflict in Industry', unpbl. M.A.Econ. thesis, Univ. of Manchester, 1960, p.v.

[4] T. Lupton, *On the Shop Floor, op. cit.*, p. 198.

tradition and a logic of sentiment. His work suggests the contrary, that 'workers behave reasonably in the light of their position in industry and society, and take steps to protect these interests wherever circumstances make this possible'.[1] Doris Arran, who reviewed the post-war literature on industrial sociology, argues in fact that much of the research has been carried out within a framework based on the value premises of management, and that this framework needs to be altered, in future research, to take cognisance of the standpoint of the workers.[2]

John Goldthorpe also criticises the attempt to explain workers' attitudes and behaviour purely in intra-organizational terms. He suggests that non-work aspects such as social and geographical mobility, the worker's position in the life-cycle, and his patterns of family and community life are relevant factors for the understanding of his orientation in the work situation. As Goldthorpe says, 'the industrial sociologist cannot allow his investigation to end "at the factory gates"'. The life of the enterprise should not be studied entirely in system terms without reference to the structure of the wider society in which the enterprise exists.[3]

Shifting our attention from the workplace to the worker in the more general setting we find Zweig's study, for instance, which sets out the new trends that have developed in the 'affluent society'. Although his investigation was concerned with factory workers—and Zweig does say that his conclusions

[1] *ibid.*, p. 201.

[2] Doris Arran, 'A Critical Examination of the Assumptions in Some Post-war British Industrial Sociology', unpbl. M.A. thesis, Univ. of Leeds, 1961, p. 142.

[3] John H. Goldthorpe, 'Attitude and Behaviour of Car Assembly Workers', *British Journal of Sociology*, vol. 17, no. 3, Sept. 1966, pp. 240–1. See also a discussion of the effects of functional specialization and bureaucratization on orientation to work, by G. K. Ingham, 'Organizational Size Orientation to Work and Industrial Behaviour', *Sociology*, vol. 1, no. 3, 1967.

apply with greater force to such workers, particularly where they come from large-scale well-organized establishments in progressive expanding fields—the author maintains that the new forces he has uncovered 'are potentially at work in every domain of working-class existence'.[1] These new tendencies can be summarized under the following headings: (a) security-mindedness; (b) rising expectations and the rise in acquisitive instincts; (c) family-mindedness and home-centredness. Zweig adds that the concomitant effects of the above trends are the 'feminization' of the worker; his diminishing interest in his mates and the struggles of his class; and his quest for respectability. Zweig's results point to a deep transformation taking place in the very ethos of the working class. This change is bringing about a situation in which 'the cleavages between classes in economic terms are fast breaking down'. Finally, Zweig points out, however, that 'new cleavages are being erected, namely cleavages of education and culture'.[2] The affluent society, according to him, has not enlarged the workers' cultural horizon.

I. C. Cannon also considered the effects that material conditions can have on the ethos of the working man. His study, which deals with the compositor in London, explains why, despite the fact that in this trade material conditions were better than among skilled workers in general, there has been strong identification with the labour movement. It appears that due to instability experienced by this skilled labour, at one period of its history, a radical ethos developed which subsequently came to be maintained by the occupational community or culture.[3] David Lockwood's study of clerical workers clarifies the trends in the class identification

[1] F. Zweig, *op. cit.*, p. 205.

[2] *ibid.*, p. 211.

[3] I. C. Cannon, *op. cit.*, esp. p. 217. See also his 'Ideology and Occupational Community: a Study of Compositors', *Sociology*, vol. 1, no. 2, May 1967.

of this occupation. First he shows that the market work and status situations of the clerk differed in the last century from that of the manual worker. Although propertyless, the clerk was not really 'proletarian', enjoying higher income, better job security and greater mobility. In his work situation he was closer to his employer than to the manual workers; he was cut off from the latter, scattered in small offices and prone to greater individualistic aspirations. His better education and middle-class style of life ensured a higher status for him. Considering these factors Lockwood refutes the theory that the clerks are an example of an occupational group which had a 'false' class consciousness, in that they did not identify with the 'labour movement'. Furthermore, he shows that as the work situation has changed for large numbers of clerks in more recent times, in that when run on a large scale and employing bureaucratic methods the modern office tends to be less paternalistic, the effect has been precisely a spread of unionization and an identification with the 'labour movement'.[1]

R. M. Blackburn, in addition, stresses that basically the reasons for trade unionism among white-collar workers are the same as for manual workers, a realization that there is a conflict of interest between worker and management. Nevertheless the conditions for unionism and its extent can vary in degree. The position is further complicated by the fact that 'the level of unionization can be represented by varying proportions of unionateness (the measure of character) and completeness (the proportion of potential membership recruited)'.[2]

Conclusions such as those of Zweig, mentioned above, have

[1] David Lockwood, *The Blackcoated Worker*, *op. cit.*, esp. conclusions, p. 201ff.

[2] R. M. Blackburn and K. Prandy, 'White-collar Unionisation', *British Journal of Sociology*, June 1965, p. 119. See also R. M. Blackburn, *Union Character and Social Class*, Batsford, 1967.

been challenged by some sociologists. Thus, John Westergaard argues against the acceptance of the thesis that a
convergence of social classes is taking place. But although he
shows that there is no continuous trend towards income
equalization or the wide diffusion of property,[1] he accepts that
the nature of the class structure is changing in that the working
class is increasingly accepting the middle-class 'yardstick' of
material achievements. He contends, however, that 'doubt
arises, not about the general truth of such observations, but
about their interpretation'.[2] His main point is that as the
levels of aspiration are continually raised, these will come to be
beyond the reach of the bulk of the population, the effect of
which is not likely to be a lessening of the cleavages between
classes[3] as Zweig maintains. Zweig's attempt to show that
certain changes have occurred in the life patterns and aspirations of the working class, changes which drive them towards
'middle classness', is also contradicted by the preliminary
research findings of the study of 'a critical sample of affluent
workers'.[4] The researchers, John Goldthorpe and associates,
contend that 'In order to achieve a high level of income, many
of these men must experience greater deprivation in their
working lives than do most white-collar employees; they also
differ from the latter in having little chance of occupational
advancement. In their home lives, they are largely "pri-
vatized". They no longer share in traditional patterns of
working-class sociability, yet few have adopted middle-class

---

[1] J. H. Westergaard, 'The Withering Away of Class: A Contemporary
Myth' in *Towards Socialism*, Fontana Library/*New Left Review*, 1965, pp.
80ff and 83.

[2] *ibid.*, p. 87. See also the section on Social Stratification.

[3] *ibid.*, p. 108.

[4] See John Goldthorpe, David Lockwood, Frank Bechofer and Jennifer
Platt, 'The Affluent Worker and the Thesis of Embourgeoisement:
Some Preliminary Research Findings', *Sociology*, vol. 1, no. 1, Jan. 1967,
p. 11.

life styles and fewer still have become assimilated into middle-class society'.

Cotgrove maintains that in British research too much emphasis has been put on social class as a variable. This has resulted in rather generalized descriptions of working-class life, for instance, without an attempt to consider the variations within class groups due to the 'differences in market, status, and work situations' which manifest themselves in different occupations.[1] There have been, however, just a few studies of particular occupations which specially emphasize their effects on family life, leisure, and political attitudes. Dennis, Henriques and Slaughter show how the miner engaged in dangerous work which needs close cooperation from his fellow workers becomes steeped in trade union brotherhood, his leisure time is spent with his mates in long periods of weekend drinking, and he takes little interest in his wife or family.[2] Jeremy Tunstall, who studied distant-water fishermen, pointed out that the three months of leisure spent ashore provide the opportunity for status seeking through conspicuous consumption. The kind of physically damaging work they carry out requires this kind of compensation, and it also leads to a belief in fate and to resignation. The long periods away from home make for little mutual understanding between husband and wife.[3] Peter Hollowell, who studied the long-distance lorry-driver, shows how this kind of occupation leads to an individualistic outlook with an emphasis on autonomy. Unlike the miner, the lorry driver dislikes unionization, but like both the miner and the fisherman his relations within the family are disturbed. Due to night work he is also alienated from the community.[4]

[1] Cotgrove, *op. cit.*, p. 143.
[2] N. Dennis, F. Henriques and C. Slaughter, *Coal is our Life*, Eyre & Spottiswoode, 1956.
[3] J. Tunstall, *The Fisherman*, MacGibbon & Kee, 1962.
[4] Peter Hollowell, *The Lorry-Driver*, Routledge, 1968.

In some sociological analyses of occupations attention is largely focused on their structure and on changes in it. In this connection a number of interesting findings are reported, especially as regards the relationship of the occupation to the rest of society. In reviewing the legal profession, Abel-Smith and Stevens argue that the easy attainment of affluence through conveyancing and probate work meant that while solicitors gave limited service to the middle classes, they neglected the more exacting service that big business required, as well as the less remunerative task of providing a 'social service' for the working classes, and so were isolated both from business and industry and from the man in the street. The former turned to accountants and other business advisers, and the latter mainly to official bodies. These developments resulted in the 'real danger that at least much of the rationale for the existence of the profession might shortly disappear'. In the meantime, the solicitor came in for much criticism for the high costs levied on clients and the poor service provided.[1]

In connection with the occupation of policemen, Michael Banton stressed the fundamental point 'that harmonious police-public relations depend to a significant extent upon the interrelation between the policeman's occupational role and his private roles. It is the policeman's participation in the society which most affects the way he exercises his powers. But his job prevents him from taking part in ordinary social relations with quite the freedom allowed to members of most occupational groups. If policemen are too detached, too much identified with criminal proceedings, relations with the public deteriorate. If they are insufficiently detached, they cannot do their work properly'.[2] This dilemma has serious implications for the way in which the occupational tasks of the policeman

[1] B. Abel-Smith and R. Stevens, *Lawyers and the Courts*, Heinemann, 1967, pp. 402–5.

[2] M. Banton, *The Policeman in the Community*, Tavistock, 1964, p. 267.

may be carried out, as well as the way in which the policeman will fit into the society in which he works.

Finally, sociologists in Britain have given some attention also to occupational mobility as distinct from social-class mobility (which will be treated below). Thus S. R. Parker showed that bank workers had little retrospective mobility by comparison with youth employment and child care officers. The past occupations of the latter were mainly the kind that involved contact with clients, whilst in the case of the bank worker a varied occupational history was not an advantage. On the whole Parker concluded that occupation itself is 'the major factor in determining the number of previous jobs'.[1] Influence on labour mobility in general seems to be exerted more by occupation than industry. In other words workers, even when changing from one industry to another, tend to stay in the same occupational group.[2] The geographical aspect of labour mobility seems to be strongly influenced by class factors, as a recent survey shows.[3]

Turning to the study of leisure activities we find a dearth of British material, although a few researches, connecting up at times with some studies in other countries, have given us some tentative results. Thus, S. R. Parker distinguishes between three main patterns of leisure. First, there is the *extension* pattern where non-work and work activities have strong connections as in the case of professional and academic people,

[1] S. R. Parker, 'Retrospective "Bridging" of Three Occupational Groups', *Sociology*, vol. 1, no. 1, Jan. 1967, p. 81. See also J. Whittaker, 'Parker on Retrospective Bridging', *ibid.*, vol. 2.

[2] G. Thomas, *Labour Mobility in Great Britain, 1945–1949, op. cit.* See also S. R. Parker *et al.*, *The Sociology of Industry, op. cit.* This book contains a number of other basic points regarding this topic, e.g. the factors of family ties, community attachment and material inducements are chief determinants of the rate of mobility. It also contains a reference to managerial mobility (see p. 29ff, 96ff and ch. 12).

[3] See S. Cotgrove and C. Jansen, *Social Aspects of Internal Migration*, Bath University, 1968.

who find their work highly satisfying and for whom work is of central interest.[1] Second, there is the *neutrality* pattern where leisure becomes of central interest because of the monotonous nature of work as with clerks and semi-skilled workers who accordingly tend to become more home-centred. Third, there is the *opposition* pattern where work is again not of central interest but where leisure is sharply cut off from work which is alienating.[2] This produces a seeking of leisure for recuperative purposes, particularly in the case of unskilled manual workers or those in extreme occupations.

Some details of the influence of one such extreme occupation on leisure activities are worth mentioning. Dennis and his co-researchers described conditions in a mining community where the almost sole source of employment, which provided jobs exclusively for men, tended to segregate them from women both in the work and the non-work situation. 'Institutional leisure activities are predominantly for males, and there is virtual or definite exclusion of women from many social activities'. But both the form and the content of leisure activities are influenced. Thus the authors suggest that 'the essentially frivolous character of leisure . . . is closely related to the insecurity both physical and social, produced in the past and present by coalmining as an occupation in Britain'.[3]

Sociologists have paid some special attention to leisure among young people. A survey in Cardiff showed that youth there splits into two main groups: those with grammar school or youth club background whose leisure activities emphasize an interest in hobbies, competitive games, outdoor life, travel and organized religion; and those without such back-

---

[1] S. R. Parker *et al.*, *op. cit.*, pp. 164, 165.
[2] A Marxist interpretation of the alienating nature of work is given in a book which brings together personal accounts from a number of occupations—see Ronald Fraser (ed.), *Work*, Penguin, 1968.
[3] Dennis *et al.*, *op. cit.*, p. 248.

grounds who prefer individual passive types of leisure, such as frequenting the cinema or television viewing. The authors suggest that the grammar-school or club background re-inforces rather than *creates* the interest shown by young people.[1] Attention has also been drawn to the fact that increas-ing leisure time among young people has led to a 'youth culture'.[2]

More generally, A. Giddens claims that the lack of interest in the analysis of leisure, a fact we mentioned above, has been due to the existence of values which have stressed the central importance of work in people's lives. But Giddens believes that 'the ever-decreasing length of the average working day suggests that problems of leisure will increasingly come into the forefront of both theoretical and practical interest'.[3]

SOCIAL STRATIFICATION AND MOBILITY

It is easy to see that social stratification is related to many other institutional aspects of society, and a number of these relationships are dealt with in other sections of this chapter, where we report for instance on sociological research in educa-tion or politics. Here we are principally concerned with the way in which British sociologists have defined and analysed social stratification, and we also pay attention to research about elites and social mobility.

[1] A. Crichton, E. James and J. Wakeford, 'Youth and Leisure in Cardiff, 1960', *Sociological Review*, vol. 10, no. 2, July 1962, p. 218.

[2] B. D. Davies and A. Gibson, *The Social Education of the Adolescent*, U.L.P., 1967, pp. 74, 75. See also a mainly psychological discussion of problems of leisure in adolescence, by D. Miller, 'Leisure and the Adolescent', *New Society*, 9 June 1966.

[3] A. Giddens, 'Notes on the Concepts of Play and Leisure', *Sociological Review*, vol. 12, no. 1, 1964, p. 87. In connection with play activities N. Elias and E. Dunning have stressed the need to revitalize 'small-group theory': see their 'Dynamics of Group Sports with Special Reference to Football', *British Journal of Sociology*, vol. 17, no. 4, Dec. 1966.

First, we shall look briefly at some conclusions reached by T. H. Marshall, who analysed social stratification in a wide and theoretical context. Marshall, who examined changes in social stratification in Europe, particularly western Europe and the United States in the twentieth century, contends that if we look at the Weberian trilogy of class, status and power we discover that there has been 'a detachment of class from stratification'. That is to say, class in the Marxist sense has weakened because 'the operative interest-groups are no longer determined by the social relationships within the system of production, that is primarily by property'.[1] But this weakening of class, or rather its change in character, holds, Marshall says, only when considered in the light of Marxist explanation. Hence economic interest groups are still important, particularly from the point of view of power relations, but these elements in the social structure no longer adequately reflect the system of stratification, particularly if we consider that social differences *between* groups may not be much greater now than *within* groups. Regarding the dimension of social status, Marshall concludes that this too has not increased in its importance. Finally, he does not see a fusion of the various dimensions to produce a ruling class or unified power elite. There does appear to be a concentration of political and administrative personnel whose origins are the middle ranks of society, but this is hardly a ruling class.[2] On the whole, Marshall maintains that 'the clear cut lines of stratification are fading', at least partly because of the emergence of all kinds of new social groupings, such as the hierarchies of entertainment celebrities built up through the mass media, giving rise to stratifications which do not fit the class dimension and do not fit easily even the pattern of social status.[3]

[1] T. H. Marshall, *Sociology at the Crossroads*, Heinemann, 1963, p. 145.
[2] *ibid.*, p. 139.
[3] *ibid.*, pp. 136, 137.

The fading of stratification lines, particularly the class dimension, appears to be substantiated by detailed findings, such as those provided by Mark Abrams for Britain. He concludes that class differences have become more confused due to the following main factors: (a) working-class affluence; (b) many new occupations do not fit easily the old classifications; (c) differences in speech and dress have greatly diminished under the impact of the mass media; (d) wider access to higher education and increased opportunities for social mobility. Abrams maintains that class differences are being replaced by differences related to age and the stages in the family life-cycle, so that working- and middle-class teenagers may have more in common with each other than with their respective middle-age groups.[1] We have already[2] mentioned similar arguments put forward by writers such as F. Zweig, that working-class affluence has led to 'middle-classness' and hence that class cleavages have been lessened. Marshall himself has also pointed to the equalizing effect that the spread of citizenship rights has had on social stratification.[3]

A number of sociologists, however, have adduced some evidence and have put forward a number of arguments in an attempt to qualify these findings. Thus R. M. Titmuss has drawn attention to the gross imperfections of the welfare state and has distinguished between the three broad categories of 'social welfare', 'fiscal welfare' and 'occupational welfare'. He went on to claim that taxation arrangements and occupational opportunities are such that they penalize the working class to the extent of counteracting the equalizing tendencies of the social services.[4] Again, it is contended that as far as

[1] M. Abrams, *The Newspaper Reading Public of Tomorrow*, Odhams, 1964, pp. 57, 58.
[2] See above, p. 152f.
[3] *op. cit.*, ch. 4.
[4] R. M. Titmuss, *Essays on 'The Welfare State'*, Allen & Unwin 1958. See also his *Income Distribution and Social Change*, Allen & Unwin 1962.

aspiration and styles of life are concerned, the gap between the lower and upper strata of society is not closing.[1] Furthermore, in regard to property ownership and concentration there is evidence to show that the nation's wealth is largely owned by a fairly small minority[2] and that effective control of the country's economic life is in the hands of the few—for instance, through interlocking directorships.[3] Ralph Miliband sums up the situation by saying that the members of the economic power elite are mainly drawn from the traditional middle and upper classes, with a sprinkling of representatives from the professional classes and some who started lower down the scale. He does not, therefore, regard the elite in Britain as hereditary but as semi-hereditary.[4] According to Miliband, although this elite naturally has social and political facets, it is in fact one economically-based governing class as understood in the Marxist sense. As Bottomore stresses, this does not allow for the possibility of the political system playing the role of 'basis', the basis being always the economic system, all other aspects being merely parts of the 'super-structure'.[5] Guttsman who carried out an exhaustive study of elites in British society, and particularly of the British political elite, also recognizes the interlocking of the various elite groups, but unlike Miliband he does not stress the exclusively economic 'basis' of the top echelons of society. He merely shows that a 'ruling class' exists in Britain, 'which provides the majority of those who occupy positions of power, and who, in their turn, can materially assist *their* sons to

[1] See above, p. 156.

[2] See some details in S. Cotgrove, *op. cit.*, p. 212.

[3] M. Barratt Brown, 'The Controllers', in *Universities and Left Review*, nos. 5, 6, 7, 1958–59.

[4] Ralph Miliband, 'Who Governs Britain?', in *Universities and Left Review*, no. 3, 1958. See also Robin Blackburn, 'Inequality and Exploitation', in *New Left Review*, no. 42, March/April 1967, p. 3ff.

[5] T. B. Bottomore, *Sociology, op. cit.*, p. 191; see also his *Elites and Society*, Watts, 1964.

reach similar positions'.[1] This class, although it still contains members of the aristocracy and descendants of the elite of former times, now also includes new groups of decision makers. The ruling class or 'power elite' still consists, however, of a narrow circle of leaders who dominate most aspects of society's life.[2]

On the whole, there is not enough empirical evidence to clarify some of the crucial issues in the above controversy. A number of studies, though, have been completed showing a persistence of elite domination and of social distance among classes. Thus T. J. H. Bishop in his study of public-school pupils shows that 'almost all Wykehamists make their careers at the professional high administrative level and a large proportion complete their careers in the grade we call elite'.[3] The wish to maintain a distance from the lower class by those higher up the scale comes out clearly in Peter Collison's study of a physical barrier set up to maintain class differences. 'The desire to retain the walls [Cutteslowe in Oxford] was not motivated solely by a concern about traffic but . . . there was also some concern about social differences between the estates and a desire for segregation from the Cutteslowe people'.[4] And John Goldthorpe maintains that there is evidence to suggest that ' "social" barriers [are] still widely existing between "working class" and "middle class" even in cases where immediate material differences have now disappeared'.[5] The controversy which has been set out above remains unresolved. Whilst most British sociologists agree that some changes have

[1] W. L. Guttsmann, *The British Political Elite*, MacGibbon & Kee, 1965, p. 356.

[2] *ibid.*, ch. 11, esp. pp. 356–9.

[3] T. J. H. Bishop, 'Origins and Achievements of Winchester College Pupils, 1836–1934', ph.d. thesis, Univ. of London, 1962, p. 358.

[4] P. Collison, *op. cit.*, p. 170.

[5] J. H. Goldthorpe, 'Social Stratification in Industrial Society', *Sociological Review Monograph 8*, Keele, 1964, p. 107.

taken place in the social stratification of British society, especially if one considers the rise of a multitude of status groupings, including localized status systems,[1] which cut across the simple Marxist class dichotomy, some would argue that the basic divisions in society have remained the same and are pinned to economic power reflected in vast inequalities of property ownership which are largely vested in a 'pluto-aristocracy'.[2]

We shall now turn to the guide British sociologists have given regarding the way in which we can define contemporary social class in Britain and the criteria upon which we can base investigations of the class system. D. G. MacRae refers to 'a system of ranks' which emanates from the assigning of statuses to human beings, the ranking being 'in terms of variables socially ascribed or individually achieved in purely socially defined contexts' and 'the only ultimate sanction [being] economic, though it may be expressed and mediated in a variety of ways'.[3] He further points out that, although British society contains elements of caste and estate, it is 'above all a society based on class'. Many sociologists have pointed to the possibility of investigating the social-class system of a society either by means of objective or subjective criteria. The objective criteria may be 'relation to the production process, source of income [or] occupation' and they 'may be observed and measured with some degree of objectivity'.[4] On the subjective side, the criterion may be one where we say that 'a person's class is simply what that person supposes it to be or declares it to be when he is asked'.[5]

---

[1] See D. E. G. Plowman, W. E. Minchinton and Margaret Stacey, 'Local Social Status in England and Wales', *Sociological Review*, vol. 10, no. 2, July 1962.

[2] R. Miliband, *op. cit.*, p. iv.

[3] D. G. MacRae, *Ideology and Society*, Heinemann, 1961, pp. 65, 66.

[4] J. B. Montague, *Class and Nationality*, Vision Press, 1963, p. 42.

[5] G. D. H. Cole, *Studies in Class Structure*, Routledge, 1955, p. 3.

F. M. Martin used the subjective criterion in a survey of Greenwich and Hertford and found that a very high percentage attempted a self-assessment. The bulk of respondents assigned themselves to the middle class and the working class.[1] It was also apparent that there was a gradual reduction, as one passed down the occupational scale, in the percentages who allocated themselves to the upper middle class, and this was also generally true of the middle class. At the same time, there was a corresponding increase in the percentages allocating themselves to the lower middle and working classes. But both in Martin's study and in that of Young and Willmott[2] sizeable groups of 'deviants' were found—for instance, groups of respondents who belonged to manual occupations but regarded themselves as belonging to the middle class. Cotgrove points out that, whilst such studies show that it is generally accepted that society is divided into social classes, there is no unanimity regarding inclusions into these classes. Furthermore, he stresses that 'Existing researches do not tell us the degree of importance which respondents attach to their class identity'.[3]

The objective criterion of occupation, the Hall–Jones scale, was used in a major study of social mobility in Britain.[4] This has been accepted as the most important single criterion and most useful index of social status. As Glass points out, 'in our society . . . occupation reflects the combined influence of

[1] Only two respondents put themselves at the very top of the scale and no more than nine per cent at the very bottom of the scale, whilst 42.5 per cent thought they belonged to the middle class and 36.6 per cent to the working class. A total of 96.1 per cent attempted a self-assessment. The survey was carried out in 1950. See F. M. Martin in D. V. Glass (ed.), *Social Mobility in Britain*, *op. cit.*, p. 51ff.
[2] M. Young and P. Willmott, 'Social Grading by Manual Workers', *British Journal of Sociology*, vol. 7, no. 4, Dec. 1956.
[3] S. Cotgrove, *op. cit.*, p. 219.
[4] D. V. Glass (ed.), *Social Mobility in Britain*, *op. cit.*

a number of factors linked with social status'.[1] Glass and his associates focused attention on inter-generational trends, G. Thomas on intra-generational mobility[2] and a number of other studies on the social origins of persons in particular occupations.[3]

We cannot do better here than give in some detail the brief summary of the findings of the above studies, provided by David Lockwood who concludes that 'the following general relationships appear to be fairly clearly established'. 'There is a considerable amount of short-range movement between adjacent occupational levels. In the study by Glass it was found that in none of the seven occupational status groups was the majority of sons to be found in the same position as that held by their fathers; and that in the sample as a whole, the proportion of sons with the same status as their fathers was roughly one-third. As far as longer-range movement is concerned, one-fifth of the sons of the highest group, professional and high administrative workers, was downwardly mobile into manual or routine non-manual jobs; and a similar proportion of the sons in the latter category rose to positions in the non-manual grades proper, mostly into positions of middle and subordinate status. The greatest opportunities for movement on the part of sons of manual workers are of necessity within the range of manual skills. This pattern is confirmed by Thomas's study of labour mobility, and by the other more specific studies, which show clearly also that lower white-collar employment is the main avenue of upward mobility out of the manual working class and that the sons of clerical workers have markedly higher chances of

[1] *ibid.*, p. 6.

[2] G. Thomas, *Labour Mobility in Great Britain, 1945–1949* (Government Social Survey), Ministry of Labour and National Service, S.S. 134.

[3] See, e.g., R. K. Kelsall, *Higher Civil Servants in Britain*, Routledge, 1955; R. V. Clements, *Managers*, Allen & Unwin, 1958; G. H. Copeman, *Leaders of British Industry*, Gee, 1955.

upward mobility than the sons of manual workers'.[1] Lockwood adds that the fact that most of the interchange is within the manual group and between this and the lower white-collar groups is understandable in view of the occupational structure in which these groups provide by far the greater proportion of all employment possibilities.

Another index of social mobility, the ecological aspect of social differentiation, has for long been noted by sociologists,[2] but little used in British research. Changes in residential pattern are closely linked with socio-economic status at the base of which is occupation. However, the fact that spatial distance affects social distance[3] is in itself important enough to make the ecological index a useful guide to trends in social mobility. It is in this vein that the present writer investigated the mobility of a group of London Jews and traced their socially ascending residential route out of the East End through north and north-west London and finally to the suburb of Edgware. This move was closely linked to the rise into higher occupational categories.[4]

The migrations of members of the elite and their monopoly of power in all kinds of community in Britain is brought out in F. Musgrove's study. He emphasizes in particular the widespread mobility, both upwards and outwards, of these leading members of society and says that 'the evidence suggests . . . that big cities as well as small towns may make abundant use of imported ability at the highest levels of employment; and that voluntary associations may enjoy the advantages of this

[1] D. Lockwood, 'Social Mobility', in A. T. Welford *et al.*, *Society*, *op. cit.*, p. 512.

[2] See, e.g., D. V. Glass, *The Town*, John Lane, 1935, p. 72.

[3] In this connection it is interesting to consider the social distance that people of different social classes maintain when they live adjacently. See, e.g., Collison, *op. cit.*, quoted above; also Willmott and Young, *Family and Class in a London Suburb*, *op. cit.*, esp. ch. 11.

[4] E. Krausz, 'A Sociological Field Study of Jewish Suburban Life in Edgware 1962–3', unpbl. PH.D. thesis, Univ. of London, 1965, p. 94.

talent to a greater extent than it has been commonly supposed.'[1] Musgrove's work also shows that the mobility described creates difficult problems of adjustment and he proposes that educational institutions should do more to prepare future members of the elite for their functions in society. In a study carried out in Bristol, S. Cotgrove and C. Jansen similarly show that mobility from one part of the country to another is directly related to occupation and education. Their report indicates that 'rates of migration were found to be three times higher among professionals than among semi-skilled and unskilled workers' and that migrants had on the whole much better educational background than residents.[2] There is much research to be done yet to show the interrelationships between different variables, family links and backgrounds, educational and occupational opportunities, residential opportunities, and their effects on social mobility.

THE SOCIOLOGY OF POLITICS

Angus Stewart distinguishes between two main approaches which characterize research in this field: the 'behavioural' and the 'systemic'.[3] The former is represented chiefly by voting studies and the latter by attempts to establish sociological frameworks for the study of politics. A number of studies fall squarely into these categories, as we illustrate below, but others fit Stewart's dichotomy less rigidly. As an example of the systemic approach we can take H. V. Wiseman's work, in which he emphasized the need to produce sociological frameworks for analysing political life. He expresses this clearly

[1] F. Musgrove, *op. cit.*, p. 70.
[2] S. Cotgrove and C. Jansen, *Social Aspects of Internal Migration*, Bath University, 1968, pp. 2, 3.
[3] Angus W. G. Stewart, 'Political Sociology: Some Approaches and Problems', *British Journal of Sociology*, vol. 18, no. 3, Sept. 1966, p. 312.

when he says: 'Ample material is readily available . . . on such problems as voting habits, pressure groups, political parties, bureaucracies and ideology. But when it is desired to fit these patterns of political behaviour into a broader and more generalized study of whole political systems, or of political sub-systems in the total social system of society . . . difficulties arise'.[1] He proceeds, therefore, to provide an exposition of Parsons' structural–functional model through which both the interaction between the polity and other institutional spheres may be studied and the functional dynamics of the political sub-system itself may be subjected to investigation.[2] System building as a prerequisite for empirical research about political phenomena is the main preoccupation of a number of workers in this field.[3]

This contrasts sharply with the 'behavioural' studies, particularly where these regard 'the study of attitudes and opinions . . . as an end in itself without systematic reference to any wider framework'.[4] The altogether non-sociological opinion polls are the best examples of such studies. Even if these predict successfully the political behaviour of the electorate they do not *ipso facto* explain such behaviour.[5] On the other hand, as Angus Stewart points out, 'The more sociological (as against attitudinal) of the voting studies have proceeded by the establishment of correlations of varying coefficients between particular variables (e.g. voting patterns and socio-economic categories) presumably on the assumption that such correlations will in time lead to theories of political behaviour'.[6]

[1] H. V. Wiseman, *Political Systems: Some Sociological Approaches*, Routledge, 1966, p. vii.

[2] *ibid.*, pp. 97, 132.

[3] For American work, see W. J. M. MacKenzie, *Politics and Social Science*, Penguin, 1967, pp. 86–110.

[4] Stewart, *op. cit.*, p. 313.

[5] W. G. Runciman, *Social Science and Political Theory*, C.U.P., p. 90ff.

[6] Stewart, *op. cit.*, p. 313.

J. Blondel who brings together a good deal of the results in this field illustrates well the establishment of such correlations. He concludes, for instance, that the important cleavages between the electors of the two major political parties are based on the broad images of the parties and that these images are associated with particular socio-economic groups: the non-manual group with the Conservatives, the unionized manual with Labour, but that there is no clear association in the case of the non-unionized manual group.[1] Conclusions such as these are based on more detailed voting studies. One of the earlier studies carried out in Greenwich (in 1949–50) by Mark Benney and his colleagues stated that 'for most voters, and in particular for working class voters, party policy plays a smaller part in attracting or repelling support than the class character of the party's public image'.[2]

There is substantial agreement that, as Richard Pear says, 'class is the most important single determinant of political behaviour'.[3] John Bonham has argued that, broadly speaking in the political context, a simple class dichotomy has to be recognized: the working class who are the manual workers and the middle class composed of the rest.[4] The complicating factor is that people may not align themselves politically according to their objective class position but rather according to their subjective class identification. Hence working-class affluence has been regarded as a major factor in the prevalence of Conservative governments in Britain in the 1950s. But although a study by Mark Abrams showed that part of the working-class vote went to the Conservative party,[5] there is

[1] J. Blondel, *Votes, Parties and Leaders*, Penguin, 1963, pp. 68, 251.

[2] Mark Benney and Phyllis Geiss, 'Social Class and Politics in Greenwich', *British Journal of Sociology*, vol. 1, no. 4, Dec. 1950, p. 323. See also Mark Benney et al., *How People Vote*, Routledge, 1956.

[3] Richard H. Pear, 'Political Parties and Elections', in Welford, *Society, op. cit.*, p. 555.

[4] John Bonham, *The Middle Class Vote*, Faber, 1954, p. 53.

[5] M. Abrams and R. Rose, *Must Labour Lose?*, Penguin, 1960.

doubt whether greater affluence in the working class leads *ipso facto* to lack of support for the Labour party. The study referred to above concludes that 'The acquisition by manual workers and their families of relatively high incomes and living standards' does not appear, according to the evidence, to be conducive to 'a political shift to the right, or in any way incompatible with a continuing high level of support for Labour'.[1] The implications for political sociology of such findings are important. For as the researchers say, 'politics has never been reducible to a mere epiphenomenon of economic conditions' but must be understood in the context of social stratification, which itself is not simply determined by the income or possessions of members of a group, 'but rather by their characteristic life-chances and experiences and by the nature of their relationships with other groups'. And this is 'a context which changes more slowly than the relative levels of wages and salaries or patterns of consumption'.[2]

Frank Parkin's thesis concerning working-class Conservatism inverts the usual explanation of this phenomenon. He argues that it is not those who vote Conservative that must be regarded as deviant, since they merely conform to the prevalent value system of society as a whole. It is the Labour supporters, who basically reject the capitalist system and with it the existing dominant values of society, that must be regarded as evincing deviant behaviour.[3] The value of Parkin's theory lies mainly in the fact that it places the study of voting behaviour into the more general context of the social structure within which voting takes place, and as such he proposes a more truly sociological explanation.

[1] Goldthorpe, Lockwood *et al.*, *op. cit.*, p. 27.
[2] *ibid.*
[3] F. Parkin, 'Working-class Conservatives: a Theory of Political Deviance', *British Journal of Sociology*, vol. 18, no. 3, Sept. 1967, esp. pp. 281–2 and 289.

Another dimension reflecting the divisions and conflicts of political life is that which can be best described by the umbrella term of 'power relations'. We have already referred to the view that an unfair distribution of power exists when the upper class or elite is compared with the other strata in society.[1] It will suffice here to point out with Peter Worsley that power grouping and 'politics' exist both inside and outside the specialized machinery of government and that in a society like Britain the two sets of power groupings cannot be meaningfully studied in isolation.[2] This is seen clearly when we examine the existence of 'pressure groups'. These power centres, which may represent sectional interests based on major divisions in society such as employer and employee, propertied and propertyless or more recondite interests, interact with the government which represents the state, which in Weberian language is the *legitimate* power centre, or as Peter Worsley says 'the repository of ultimate legitimacy'.[3] This interaction is a necessary aspect of a mass complex society. As J. D. Stewart concludes on the basis of a thorough examination of pressure groups in Britain, without this interaction the coherent expression of opinion would be rendered impossible and discontent would grow.[4]

A number of studies have stressed, however, the fundamental consensus that prevails in political life. R. T. McKenzie's study of the distribution of power within the Conservative and Labour parties points to the fact that 'neither great party at any point has threatened to disrupt the parliamentary system in order either to impose its own policies or to prevent its opponents from implementing theirs'.[5] This

[1] See above, p. 164f.
[2] P. Worsley, 'The Distribution of Power in Industrial Society', *Sociological Review Monograph 8*, Keele, 1964, pp. 18, 30.
[3] *ibid.*, p. 18.
[4] J. D. Stewart, *British Pressure Groups*, O.U.P., 1958, p. 244.
[5] R. T. McKenzie, *British Political Parties*, Heinemann, 1955, p. 581.

shows itself in a willingness to provide the competing teams for the electorate to choose from, but always to observe the rules of the political game of parliamentary democracy. The existence of such stability has been variously explained: by T. H. Marshall in terms of the spread of citizenship rights;[1] by writers taking account of Marxist theories in terms of 'engineered' consensus by means of a 'modified dominance of the property-owning classes';[2] and by some sociologists in terms of the 'socialization' of the young, resulting in their disaffiliation from active participation in politics and the acceptance of political conservatism. Abrams and Little give the following tentative findings from a study of political activism among youth: 'There are of course continual minority flirtations with more overt forms of rebellion and these perhaps are indicative of a quite general submerged discontent. But the weight of the political system prevents this mood becoming articulate or effective'.[3] They learn the political orientations of their elders, become preoccupied with personal and domestic matters and with the wish to achieve adulthood, and are influenced by material well-being, the net result of which is a growth of indifference to politics. The researches of Abrams and Little lead them to the conclusion that 'the politics of the young demonstrate the political nonentity of youth'. This fits well into a context of stability which characterizes Britain, for de-politicizing seems to go hand in hand with the endorsement of the *status quo*.[4]

[1] See 'Citizenship and Social Class', in T. H. Marshall, *Sociology at the Crossroads, op. cit.*, ch. 4.

[2] P. Worsley, *op. cit.*, p. 22. On this point he cites Perry Anderson, 'Origins of the Present Crisis', *New Left Review*, 23, Jan./Feb. 1964, pp. 26–63.

[3] Philip Abrams and Alan Little, 'The Young Activist in British Politics', *British Journal of Sociology*, vol. 16, no. 4, p. 331ff.

[4] Abrams and Little, 'The Young Voter in British Politics', *British Journal of Sociology*, vol. 16, no. 2, p. 95.

SOCIAL CHANGE—THEORETICAL ISSUES

Quite naturally, much common ground has been covered by writers who have concentrated on the analysis of sociological theory. This is evident when one considers their work clarifying the theories of 'classical' sociologists. And the same impression is gained from the topics they discuss. Thus, the basic principles and methods involved in the scientific study of society preoccupied sociologists like Morris Ginsberg, T. H. Marshall, Donald MacRae, T. B. Bottomore, John Rex and W. J. H. Sprott. The theories regarding social change and evolution, and social stratification are similarly considered by those mentioned here. We shall now select just one topic in order to illustrate, albeit most inadequately, some of the appraisals and conclusions found in the work of these and other sociologists. As we have said, a number of them have dealt with theories of social change. This is a topic particularly rewarding for us to consider because it reveals the views of British sociologists, not only regarding the theories of social change and the positions they hold on the causation of change, but also their ideas concerning the models or schemata which should be employed in sociological research.

To Morris Ginsberg social change is 'a change in social structure, e.g. the size of a society, the composition or balance of its parts or the type of its organization'.[1] Ginsberg analysed the various factors which have been adduced for the explanation of social change: individual volition, acts on behalf of individuals and special groups of people, structural changes due, for instance, to a change in the balance of forces and structural strains or tensions caused by a lack of equilibrium between the parts of the structure, external influences through conquest or culture contact, the convergence of several ele-

---

[1] Morris Ginsberg, *Evolution and Progress*, Heinemann, 1961, p. 143.

ments derived from different sources, accidental happenings, and the emergence of a common will.[1]

In considering the mechanisms that produce social change Percy Cohen lists and clarifies seven distinct theories. These revolve around the factors or phenomena of technology, economic conditions, conflict, malintegration, adaptation, ideational conditions and cultural interaction. Cohen criticizes the search for a single theory of social change. He maintains that there can be many sources of change, and hence no single factor will adequately explain *all* social change. He links the search for a single explanatory factor to what he regards to be a false notion of a single theory of social persistence. But although he disagrees with attempts to arrive at simplified theories, he also criticizes the 'tendency for social theorists to abdicate the responsibility for locating the more important sources of social change by arguing that all factors are relevant'. Cohen argues that 'they may all be relevant, but some are more so than others', and that 'the relevance of social factors is governed by the type of change to be explained'.[2]

W. J. H. Sprott and T. B. Bottomore distinguish between two major types of theory of social change: the linear and the cyclical theories. The former, according to Sprott, allow for setbacks but portray social change as occurring in a general direction.[3] These theories, Bottomore maintains, 'had the great merit that they delineated, in one form or another, a number of significant cumulative changes in human social history: the growth of knowledge, the increasing scale and complexity of societies, and in modern times the growing movement towards social and political equality'.[4] The cyclical theories are those which, as Sprott says, 'depict social change

[1] *ibid.*, pp. 152–163.
[2] Percy S. Cohen, *Modern Social Theory*, Heinemann, 1968, p. 205.
[3] W. J. H. Sprott, *Sociology*, Hutchinson, 1949, p. 168.
[4] T. B. Bottomore, *Sociology*, Allen & Unwin, 1962, p. 274.

in terms of a circular movement, or a succession of rhythmic ups and downs'. When not confined to individual states, but used on a grander scale, Sprott points out that these theories 'seek to explain the rise and fall of whole civilizations'.[1]

The two types of theory, according to Cohen, share 'the common belief that societies pass through certain determinate stages, and that the process is an inevitable one'.[2] To delve into these problems would mean, as Cohen suggests, entering the field of the sociology of ideas. Although we do not wish to elaborate here on the question of social development or progress, Ernest Gellner's clear exposition of the major conceptions in this field is important. Thus Gellner shows that the earlier conceptions of progress were episodic: a major transition through some *one* episode from one state of affairs to another. Then followed the evolutionist theories, which 'explain and validate society in terms of a long-term, indeed permanent and all-embracing *process* and not a single episode'. This means 'a whole series of transitions'. And finally we have the neo-episodic conception which, whilst it shares with evolutionist ideas a sense of the complexity of social phenomena and of growth, does not attempt a global, all-embracing infinite and eternal explanation of human life. The episodic ideas provided an over-simplified model; society and social phenomena and their change cannot be explained by one episode, however protracted.[3] Evolutionist theories have in their earlier forms been abandoned. The reason for this may be found in Ioan Davies' view that 'The argument against evolutionary theories is not so much that they are concerned with progress or sequences of change or development, but that they purport to offer total interpretations of human

---

[1] *op. cit.*, p. 168.
[2] *op. cit.*, p. 208.
[3] Ernest Gellner, *Thought and Change*, Weidenfeld, 1964, pp. 4, 9, 42, 43.

behaviour'.[1] Nevertheless, evolutionist elements are still present in the currently accepted theories of progress and development. In general terms these show the change from simple to more complex forms of society.[2] Michael Banton adduces anthropological and sociological evidence to illustrate such developments.[3] But as both Gellner and Cohen insist, the modified evolutionary concepts must be free from biological links.[4] The theoretical discussions now seem to revolve mainly around the question of the extent to which evolutionary theories in some form or other, or rather the neo-episodic concepts of various kinds, may be useful in studying the development of industrial societies, more specifically the change from pre-industrial simpler societies to modern complex ones.[5]

Another way of looking at social change is to distinguish between long-term and short-term changes. The long-term theories, Sprott says, 'claim to establish persistent trends'.[6] The long-term theory *par excellence* is the evolutionary one.

The short-term view is one according to which 'social change . . . is determined by an accumulation of changes in various sections of social life', and Sprott recognizes these smaller-scale changes as important.[7] MacRae's conclusion is in fact that since 'Unilineal evolution is . . . exceptional and long, [and] quasi-evolutionary sequences . . . rare', in the

[1] Ioan Davies, 'The Poverty of Sociology—the Science of the Modern', *Listener*, 7 March 1968, p. 298.

[2] Cohen, *op. cit.*, pp. 221–34.

[3] Michael Banton, *Roles*, Tavistock, 1965, p. 17.

[4] Gellner, *op. cit.*, p. 43, and Cohen, *op. cit.*, p. 223. Gellner sees the modifications sufficiently basic to talk of neo-episodic concepts, as we have seen above.

[5] Ioan Davies, *op. cit.* See also N. Birnbaum, 'The Idea of Industrial Society', *Sociological Review Monograph 8, op. cit.*, and T. H. Marshall, *op. cit.*, pp. 141–9.

[6] *op. cit.*, p. 170.

[7] *ibid.*, pp. 170–1.

immediate future 'Homotaxial comparisons drawn from short sequences must . . . be the mainstay of any theory of social change'.[1]

Social change has been recognized as being a practically continuous process, and not necessarily in the evolutionary sense. According to T. H. Marshall it is partly produced by mechanisms built into the social system, e.g. legislative bodies which introduce systematic change, and partly by non-systematic elements, e.g. deviations and conflicts. It is this distinction, Marshall says, which although it exists, is difficult to pin down. The distinction is 'between change that occurs smoothly within the system without breaking it or destroying its identity, and change which attacks it and swiftly transforms it into something different'.[2] John Rex takes a different view. He puts forward the theory of conflict as a theory of social change.[3] According to him, as far as the underlying process is concerned no distinction is necessary, for all change, which indeed is a continuous process, stems basically from conflict situations. In analysing the nature of conflict he recognizes the formation of conflict groups which are organized around conflicting aspirations or aims, and then describes different possible conflict situations: the ruling class situation, the revolutionary situation and the truce situation. But all these situations are merely different ways of achieving a temporary balance of power in a constantly changing social system.[4] He contrasts this theory of conflict, which regards the conflict situation as the independent variable and, therefore, the prime progenitor of change in society, with the functionalist theory which debars any sociological theory of change 'because the whole functionalist effort is devoted to showing why things

[1] D. G. MacRae, *Ideology and Society*, Heinemann, 1961, p. 147.
[2] *op. cit.*, p. 31.
[3] John Rex, *Key Problems of Sociological Theory*, Routledge, 1961, p. 131.
[4] *ibid.*, ch. 7.

are as they are'. Bottomore also points out that 'Much recent sociology, under the influence of functionalism, has disregarded problems of change or has presented them in such a way as to suggest that social change is something exceptional. The emphasis has been upon the stability of social systems and of systems of values and beliefs, and upon consensus rather than diversity and conflict within each society.' But he argues that societies are characterized by both continuity and change, the former maintained by social control, especially education, and the latter promoted by the growth of knowledge and social conflict.[1] It may also be noted that, whilst Rex's theory of conflict appears fundamentally to be a monocausal theory, Ginsberg's analysis and Cohen's views, mentioned above, emphasize that we must recognize a plurality of causes in social change.

Suggestions for research frameworks and areas to be investigated have been proposed on the basis of conclusions reached regarding theories of social change. Thus Rex outlines his conflict model for the purpose of the analysis of social systems. This implies: (a) a rejection of the idea that social systems are organized around a consensus of values and the acceptance of such systems involving conflict situations; (b) that such situations produce not a unitary but a plural society; (c) that usually there will be an unequal balance of power; (d) that the power situation may change; (e) the possibility of dramatic changes in the balance of power, e.g. where a subject class may destroy a former ruling class; (f) that the social institutions and culture of the subject class are geared to the class's interest in the conflict situation; and (g) that a change in the balance of power may lead not to complete revolution but to compromise and reform.[2] Rex puts forward the above as a useful framework for analysing contemporary social situations. He says: 'The classification of basic conflict situations, the study of the

[1] Bottomore, *op. cit.*, pp. 278–9.
[2] Rex, *op. cit.*, pp. 129–30.

emergence and structure of conflict groups, the problem of the legitimation of power, the study of the agencies of indoctrination and socialization, the problem of the ideological conflicts in post-revolutionary situations and in situations of compromise and truce, the study of the relations between norms and systems of power—all these have their place within it.' And he continues: 'The model has been developed, of course, in relation to the study of total social systems and with special emphasis upon their overtly political aspects. But it is by no means without relevance to the design of research into problems of particular institutions and social segments.'[1]

Percy Cohen, who emphasizes the plurality of sources of change and the possibility of unevenness in the 'advances' made in various respects by different societies, suggests that for analysing the course of social change in a developmental manner models will have to be constructed which use a small number of factors at a time. 'The assumptions linking these factors would not necessarily be applicable to all or even a great number of the developmental stages; though a scheme of this kind would certainly make use of certain very general assumptions about the nature of social interaction, the characteristics of social systems and the likely causes of social change.'[2]

T. B. Bottomore formulated a typology of social change which, he suggests, 'would serve as a framework for comparative study, and as a basis for generalization and interpretation'. He visualizes such a typology in terms of four major problems: (1) 'Where does social change originate?' (2) 'What are the initial conditions from which large scale changes begin?' (3) 'What is the rate of change?' and (4) 'To what extent is social change fortuitous, causally determined or purposive?'[3]

[1] *ibid.*, pp. 130–1.
[2] Cohen, *op. cit.*, p. 221.
[3] Bottomore, *op. cit.*, p. 285ff.

Bottomore argues that only through the use of more precise models can an adequate analysis of social change be carried out, for this 'would make possible the formulation of problems and the systematic presentation of results'.[1]

To sum up, as far as sociological research into social change is concerned, it appears that British sociologists are first of all in favour of abandoning the preoccupation with and use of general theories concerned with long-term changes and prefer to accept the importance of short sequence changes. Secondly, they emphasize the need to carry out research with the aid of clearly set-up models or frameworks.

Finally it must be stressed that although in this section we have dealt only with the *theoretical* work of sociologists concerned with social change, much *empirical* research on social change has been carried out, some of which is mentioned elsewhere in this book. This empirical research is mainly concerned with specific situations of change either in the setting of some industries, examples being the studies of O. and J. A. Banks, W. H. Scott and others,[2] or more generally in certain communities, as exemplified by the work of Margaret Stacey in Banbury and Tom Brennan and his colleagues in Swansea.[3] Under the rubric of social change could also come the longitudinal surveys carried out by the Population Investigation Committee in conjunction with other research bodies,[4] and work done on the borderline of sociology by the

[1] *ibid.*, p. 276.

[2] J. A. Banks, *Industrial Participation, op. cit.*; O. Banks, *The Attitudes of Steel Workers to Technical Change, op. cit.*; W. H. Scott *et al., Technical Change and Industrial Relations, op. cit.*; W. H. Scott *et al., Coal and Conflict*, Liverpool U.P., 1963.

[3] M. Stacey, *Tradition and Change, op. cit.*; Tom Brennan *et al., Social Change in South-west Wales*, Watts, 1954.

[4] See J. W. B. Douglas and J. M. Blomfield, *Children under Five*, Allen & Unwin, 1958; J. W. B. Douglas, *The Home and the School*, MacGibbon & Kee, 1964; and J. W. B. Douglas *et al., All Our Future*, Davies, 1968.

Newsons at Nottingham.[1] The merit of empirical work in the area of social change is that it tends to replace the largely speculative character of theoretical research by providing some factual evidence concerning this important conceptual dimension in sociology.[2]

GENERAL COMMENTS

The overall results of sociological research in Britain are not unimpressive. The general view one gains, however, is that of a giant jigsaw puzzle with many pieces missing. Thus partial pictures have been built up which cover many areas, as evidenced by the studies of group relations or those dealing with changes in certain institutions such as the family or education. But these partial pictures, themselves incomplete, do not fit together to depict the total scene sufficiently well. This may be due to the fact that most of the researches in the various spheres have often been undertaken solely to yield results relevant to those spheres without even a secondary aim of linking up with other aspects of the total scene, i.e. with other social institutions in the social structure.

W. J. H. Sprott has already called attention to the disorderliness and undeveloped state in sociology, and given a number of reasons for such conditions. Among these were the infinite variety of fields of investigation, the difficulty of handling the subject matter due to its familiarity, the limited opportunities offered for investigations, as well as other factors.[3] But sociology is not altogether 'an unorganized hotch-potch of

[1] John and Elizabeth Newson, *Infant Care in an Urban Community*, Allen & Unwin, 1963; and by the same authors, *Four Years Old in an Urban Community*, Allen & Unwin, 1968.

[2] In connection with empirical studies of social change, see J. Banks (ed.), *Studies in British Society*, Crowell, New York, 1968.

[3] W. J. H. Sprott, *Science and Social Action*, Watts, 1954, pp. 43–56.

endeavours' as Sprott saw it in the early 1950s. The research endeavours and results, mostly added since then, suggest that the discipline is advancing along certain lines and creating a certain pattern. Witness the special fields which have developed, such as the sociology of education, the sociology of religion, the sociology of race relations, and so on. More than this, indirectly and to a limited extent there is even linkage. For instance, in studies of both education and deviant behaviour variables such as social class or aspects of family life appear, but the relationships between education and deviant behaviour, or between these and, say, religious institutions, have not been fully explored. A meaningful picture of total British society is, therefore, emerging only very slowly. Perhaps a full view and perfect understanding of the workings of a total society is unattainable. The question is whether this is because it is not legitimate to adopt an 'integralist' stance, a view taken by D. G. MacRae,[1] or that it is the methodological immaturity of the subject which places limitations on over-all results, preventing us from seeing clearly enough the way society works. Our review suggests that the latter is an important limiting factor.

It must be stressed that the metaphor used above is not meant to imply that sociological work in Britain has been only descriptive. A good deal of it has certainly been of this nature, but this is not to be decried, since description is a necessary antecedent to analysis. At the same time analytical work has also proceeded in most of the areas considered. As shown in

[1] By 'integralism' MacRae means 'a set of beliefs that involve one in claiming that social structures form a "seamless web" in which every institution and social position is linked to every other and is part of a unique, interconnected configuration. . . .' He is against such an image and argues that 'it is precisely the study of discontinuities and areas of autonomy in social structure that is one of the most promising fields in contemporary general sociology'. See Donald G. MacRae, 'The Crisis in Sociology', in J. H. Plumb (ed.), *Crisis in the Humanities*, Penguin, 1964, pp. 127, 128.

the last section, there has also been some attempt to disentangle sociological theories and thereby to provide models for future research. Such attempts should make for more integration of research undertaken in the multitude of topics. The integration must evolve in two directions: between topics and spheres of study on the one hand, and between theory and empirical work on the other. We shall return to a consideration of this latter relationship in the concluding chapter. First our attention will be turned, however, to the former type of integration, which we discuss under the general heading of 'continuity of research'.

5. Continuity of research

There are three important problems that must be faced in sociological research. There is, first, the question of continuity. By this we mean not only the organization of the type of continuous research exemplified by longitudinal surveys, important as these may be, but the whole process of erecting general frameworks of research within which special projects can proceed so as to contribute additively to the emergence of coherent results. It should be obvious that continuity, cumulativeness and coherence are inextricably intertwined. Secondly, still with 'continuity' in mind, we must consider the role of the research unit, which usually implies teamwork, as against that of the individual researcher, and assess the contributions these can make. Thirdly, since research units often have teams which include social scientists from various disciplines, the question of the value to sociology of the inter-disciplinary approach must be considered.

The importance of continuity, in the broader sense, has been stressed in connection with research in a number of areas. The Centre for Urban Studies believes that its objectives[1] 'could best be fulfilled within the framework of a coherent, long-term programme of research', and it also emphasizes that continuity 'is the single most important prerequisite for the work of a social research organization. Without it research can hardly be genuinely experimental, nor

[1] Its objectives are 'to contribute to the systematic knowledge of towns, and in particular of British towns; to carry out, to assist and to encourage comparable studies of urban development, structure and society in this country and abroad; and to link academic social research with social policy'. See Centre for Urban Studies, *Quinquennial Report for 1958 to 1962*, University College, London, p. 4.

can it achieve cumulative results in training and output.' The assumption of the maintenance of continuity meant in fact that the Centre developed its interests in that light, and it has based on the same argument its collection of material, and its organization of various studies, 'so that they follow from one another, draw upon one another, and can make joint use of the same, or related, skills and sources'.[1]

The Population Investigation Committee has exhibited its close interest in research continuity and integration in two ways. First, it has one of the finest records of cooperation with official bodies. It has shown this amply through its work to improve systematically the basic data available for the study of population questions and through its collection of new data relevant to the changing needs of demographic research.[2] Second, it has cooperated with other research units in sustaining a longitudinal survey which has already proved to be one of the most valuable contributions to the sociology of education.[3]

One can also discern very clearly an emphasis on continuity in the work of the Institute of Community Studies. After the completion of the first three projects the main strategy was to follow the leads which these produced. The Bethnal Green study, concerned with relationships between adult relatives, was followed by a similar study in Woodford, because the first study could not answer the question whether the 'extended family' was to be found in a middle-class suburban area as well as in a working-class urban area; and again another study was mounted in Bethnal Green itself in order to compare information from teenagers with the information previously obtained mostly from married people.[4] The interest in

[1] *ibid.*, pp. 4, 10.

[2] Population Investigation Committee at the London School of Economics and Political Science, *A Record of Research and Publications*, p. 7.

[3] See J. A. Banks (ed.), *Studies in British Society*, *op. cit.*, p. 180.

[4] Michael Young and Peter Willmott, 'Research Report No. 3—Institute of Community Studies', *Sociological Review*, vol. 9, no. 2, July 1961, p. 207.

working-class adolescents has continued as evidenced by another recent study of the Institute.[1]

In the field of industrial sociology Richard Brown points out that in the researches carried out at the University of Liverpool there has been at an early phase 'an explicit attempt to give the investigations unity and coherence; to show how one investigation has given rise to problems which call for another; to use a common framework of analysis; and to make the research findings cumulative'.[2]

The need for continuity and integration has been evident also in the work of other research institutes. Political and Economic Planning worked out an integrated research programme around the theme of industrial and social adaptation in Britain for the 1960s and 1970s, involving 'studies in depth lasting for several years'.[3] A similar trend is noticeable in some of the work of the Institute of Race Relations; its lengthy and large-scale survey of race relations in Britain, conducted by E. J. B. Rose, is being further supplemented by a number of specially commissioned studies and additional pieces of research.[4]

The merits of research continuity have also been stressed in connection with the work which is being carried out in the Department of Social Anthropology at the University of Edinburgh. The Department has concentrated attention on certain topics such as race relations, and on certain geographical areas as in its studies of rural communities in Scotland. Kenneth Little makes the following points: 'The presence at the same spot of a number of investigators who have worked in the same field, as well as of files and other documentation, largely off-sets difficulties of communication. . . . More ob-

---

[1] Peter Willmott, *Adolescent Boys of East London*, Routledge, 1966.

[2] Richard K. Brown, 'Participation, Conflict and Change in Industry', *Sociological Review*, vol. 13, no. 3, Nov. 1965, p. 274.

[3] See *PEP Annual Report 1962–3*, p. 10.

[4] See *The Nuffield Foundation Report 1964–5*, O.U.P., 1965, pp. 45–6.

viously the concentration of research upon a particular problem or geographical region facilitates the launching of fresh projects because a new worker can take over at a point where previous investigators left off. Also when connection is continuously and intensively maintained with the same area it greatly expedites the making of arrangements. A new project can be launched with less expense and appreciable periods of time usually spent in making initial contacts and finding informants be reduced. It also enables the area in question to be used as a training ground for younger workers.'[1]

So far as the sociology of education is concerned, Jackson and Marsden suggest that a field research unit should be established by the ministry responsible for education. They say that there is a need for regular comparative surveys from 'outside' as well as the methodical collection of data *within* the educational system. They ask: 'Should this work be left to isolated individuals who come to feel that something should be done, and discover a way of doing it?'[2] It should be pointed out that in other areas Government-sponsored research through the Social Survey has in fact been providing basic factual information, for example on labour mobility, housing, depopulation and rural life, old age, children in care and on aspects of adolescence.[3] In connection with the last topic

[1] 'This can be quite serious when, as in the case of Edinburgh, the greater proportion of anthropological and sociological colleagues and the principal libraries are located three or four hundred miles away', Kenneth Little, 'Research Report No. 2', *Sociological Review*, vol. 8, no. 2, Dec. 1960, pp. 263–4.

[2] Brian Jackson and Dennis Marsden, *Education and the Working Class*, Penguin, 1966, p. 251.

[3] See, e.g., Geoffrey Thomas, *Labour Mobility in Great Britain 1945–9*, Ministry of Labour, ss. 134; P. G. Gray and R. Russell, *The Housing Situation in 1960*, Ministry of Housing, May 1962, ss. 319; P. G. Gray and Elizabeth A. Parr, *Children in Care and the Recruitment of Foster Parents*, Home Office, Nov. 1957, ss. 249; Geoffrey Thomas and Barbara Osborne, *Older People and their Employment*, Ministry of Labour, National Service

mentioned Leslie Wilkins has pointed to the value of comprehensive, nationally extensive, basic research work in improving the local and more restricted studies. He gives an example of this: 'It has long been realized by some organizations concerned with research into problems affecting the development of young persons that such local and restricted studies would gain much in value if it could be known how representative or unrepresentative they were. For example, it has often been noted that "broken homes" occur very frequently amongst young persons convicted by the courts, yet without a knowledge of the frequency of "broken homes" amongst those not convicted the information has little meaning. Thus the "average" (a meaningless concept on its own) adds meaning to other information when compared with it.'[1]

A number of preliminary conclusions can be drawn from the examples and views adduced above. First of all, continuity of research seems to depend on the existence of some kind of research unit. Secondly, the research of such units can enhance both basic extensive knowledge and more specialized study. Thirdly, apart from the academic arguments in favour of the research unit, there are a number of material advantages that accrue to research which is not carried out by individuals in isolation. But there may also be a number of drawbacks where research is undertaken under the wings of research units. First, the continuity itself may give rise at a certain stage or in certain circumstances to the pursuit of research no longer necessary or rewarding. This may be a product of

---

Reports, 150/1 and 150/2; *Depopulation and Rural Life* (for various regions of Scotland), see Reports NS 120 etc., 1949; Leslie T. Wilkins, *The Adolescent in Britain*, a report on a nation-wide survey of younger persons between 15–19 years of age, carried out in 1950, Central Office of Information, SS. 148 (P), July 1955.

[1] Wilkins, *op. cit.*, p. 1. It may be mentioned here that medical literature now contains a number of estimates of the frequency of broken homes in controlled populations.

sheer inertia and can be obviated by a flexibly-minded leadership in the unit, which is alert to basic changes that necessitate reorientations. Secondly, the unit may exert a constraining influence on individual researchers working within it. The effect of this may be to reduce the free play of individual imagination and creativity which is an essential element in the research procedure. The extent to which such a stultifying atmosphere will prevail will depend largely on the actual set-up in the particular research unit.

It is on the grounds of the inhibiting effects of the unit on the individual researcher and on his particular flair or interest that one could justify uncoordinated research work. This kind of unplanned research is well reflected in the self-assessment made by the Department of Social Administration at the London School of Economics. The work of the Department is regarded as not constituting in any way a unified whole and as being merely 'the sum of individual interests and efforts'.[1] One can add another example of purely *ad hoc* research. The Acton Society Trust is a case in point, for according to J. A. Banks this research unit 'is guided in its choice of subjects by what it feels to be novel or threatening in the tendencies of our time'.[2] This kind of *eclectic research* contrasts sharply with the *linked research* found in most units, independent or university ones, some of which we described above.[3]

We must draw attention here to two recent developments in Britain in the social sciences generally: the Data Bank and the research register. A certain amount of progress is visible

[1] See B. Abel-Smith, 'Research Report No. 4—Department of Social Administration, London School of Economics', *Sociological Review*, vol. 10, no. 3, 1962, p. 334.

[2] J. A. Banks in *Sociologische Gids*, Boom and Meppel, Aug. 1958, p. 181.

[3] It should be noted that 'linked research' does not necessarily signify concentration on one topic alone. Most research units pursue several interests which may or may not be integrated into one major scheme.

in the units established by the Social Science Research Council in conjunction with Essex University, and by the Research and Intelligence Unit of the Greater London Council. Work in this sphere has also been carried out by the Department of Education and Science and the British Council.[1] As far as the research register is concerned, the GLC unit is devoted, in one of its main functions, to keeping contact with all research relevant to its interests. The register is not envisaged to contain actual research data, but it would have a codified record of topics of research completed or currently being carried out. This should permit the preparation of relevant reports or the rapid drawing up of a review in any field where further research is contemplated. Thus background information and some kind of guidance would be available for those seeking advice. The Data Bank on the other hand is a repository of detailed results from past researches and affords the possibility of easy retrieval. These developments would clearly aid in achieving greater coordination of research and cumulativeness of results, and it would also help to prevent unnecessary repetition of studies and *ad hoc* research which

[1] See 'SSRC Data Bank', *Social Science Research Council Newsletter 3*, May 1968. The Data Bank is concerned with information gathered in questionnaire surveys. Due to storage problems these are not fully exploited; much is lost or destroyed and is not available for secondary analysis. It is the task of the Data Bank to prevent this by storing the information on punch cards or magnetic tape, retrieval being possible by mechanical means or computer (see *ibid.*, p. 6). The first step of the Data Bank has been to introduce computerized cataloguing of survey questions producing key-word lines, which seems the most suitable system for the wide variety of expected users of the bank (see SSRC—*Data Bank Newsletters*, Oct. and Nov. 1967, and SSRC Data Bank, *Catalogue*, University of Essex, Jan. 1968). In connection with the other bodies mentioned, see *Quarterly Bulletin of the Research and Intelligence Unit*, Greater London Council, no. 1, Dec. 1967, esp. pp. 6 and 11; and *Scientific Research in British Universities and Colleges 1966/7, vol. 3: Social Sciences*, Department of Education and Science and the British Council, HMSO, 1967.

might be futile in view of existing findings and patterns of research.

The OECD report on social science research has also emphasized the urgent need for accepting the 'clearing house' scheme, and has laid the blame for its absence at least partly on social scientists themselves. It says: 'Some of them, while feeling a need for more intensive mutual contacts and a more systematic exchange of ideas and experience, do not seem to favour deep-going reorganization of the existing organizational structure, and are likely to confuse the need for coordination with a dogmatic centralization of research which would jeopardize their autonomy.' At the same time the report recognizes the problem created by lack of adequate financing. Especially, it says, 'the system of short-term contracts is directly responsible for the discontinuous non-cumulative nature of so much social research. Sponsoring bodies are reluctant to extend support to follow-up studies, to replication studies, and extensions of previous work, preferring, understandably enough, to encourage novel topics and original approaches'.[1] The absence of a special clearing house for sociological research, and the obviously urgent need for it is only beginning to be recognized.

This recognition is seen in the survey of sociological research which was carried out by the SSRC and the British Sociological Association among the latter's members and the subsequent publication of a register which contains information about past research work and present interests among members.[2] More will have to be done in this field; a fully

[1] Organization for Economic Cooperation and Development, *The Social Sciences and the Policies of Governments*, Paris, 1966, pp. 63, 64. The problem of the short-term financing of research is also brought out in a report of the Institute of Community Studies: see M. Young and P. Willmott, 'Research Report No. 3', *Sociological Review, loc. cit.*, p. 211ff.

[2] See M. P. Carter, 'Report on the Survey of Sociological Research in Britain', Univ. of Edinburgh, July 1967; and *The British Sociological Association Register*, Dec. 1967.

established clearing-house system should obviously be the aim.

Let us now turn to the second theme of this chapter: the roles of the research unit and the individual researcher working independently of the unit. A few examples of their work will help us discuss their respective roles. In two principal areas the unit with its permanent research team is the generally accepted research medium. One is the follow-up survey and the other the nation-wide survey. Some studies, such as that undertaken by J. W. B. Douglas under the auspices of the Population Investigation Committee, fulfil both these functions. A national sample of children born in 1946 were followed through their various stages of development, and follow-up studies in 1965 continued both in respect of those who were still at school or in full-time education and those who were at work.[1] Again, the student enquiry of the Sociological Research Unit at the London School of Economics, started under R. K. Kelsall and continued under Christina Holbraad, has employed a nation-wide sample as well as the follow-up survey technique.[2] One example of a large-scale enquiry currently underway which is restricted to one area but which follows-up previous studies is the *Third Survey of London Life and Labour* under the direction of Ruth Glass. The aims and orientation of this work, which is done at the Centre for Urban Studies, is summed up in the following paragraph: 'Our original research programme, prepared in 1957, included plans for such a survey, plans to carry on, though not necessarily to repeat in all respects, work done by Charles Booth in his great enquiry on *Life and*

[1] See 'The National Survey of the Health and Development of Children', Part III of *Report for the Two Years Ended 30 June 1965*, Population Investigation Committee at the London School of Economics, p. 2.

[2] See Part IV, 'Research in the London School of Economics and Political Science', in *Calendar 1962–3*, p. 525.

Labour of the People in London (published from 1889 to 1903); and followed up by the *New Survey of London Life and Labour* (published in nine volumes from 1930 to 1935). It was our intention to undertake the Third London Survey—as one of the contributions that the Centre could make towards maintaining and encouraging continuity in British urban studies. And it was thought that a sequel to the two classic London enquiries might be of interest and use well beyond the actual area of investigation: it would be an exceptional, if not unique, example of a longitudinal survey, providing both factual and methodological comparisons over time, of one of the great cities of the world.'[1] An example of a smaller-scale enquiry also using the follow-up technique is given by Margaret Stacey's study of Banbury.[2] Fifteen years after the original enquiry (in 1950) a new study is being undertaken. It is pointed out that 'The timing of the research will make it possible to test predictions made in [the first study] about ways in which the social situation would develop and also to test hypotheses suggested in that work.'[3]

Follow-up enquiries by their very nature stress the importance of the comparative method and that of focusing attention on social change. These aspects have also been highlighted in other types of linked study undertaken by research teams. Examples are the studies of family life as viewed in the social class and community contexts carried out by Michael Young and Peter Willmott at the Institute of Community Studies,[4] and the studies concerned with workers' attitudes to technical change carried out in Liverpool University.[5]

From our account of the work of research units it is

[1] Centre for Urban Studies, *Quinquennial Report, op. cit.*, pp. 29, 30.
[2] See above, p. 21.
[3] See Nuffield Foundation, *Report for the Year Ended 31 March 1966*, O.U.P., pp. 40, 41 (the study is carried out by a small team, *ibid.*, p. 41).
[4] See above, p. 18.
[5] See above, p. 32.

obvious that they have specialized mainly in empirical work. Whilst much of the work emanating from such units tends to produce 'middle-range' theories through the empirical testing of hypotheses, examples given in the previous chapter show that theoretical research, particularly in the realm of the 'grand theory', has been the domain of the individual sociologist. Perhaps the individual's *forte* is where theoretical research is involved; and similarly the unit has advantages where large-scale empirical research is undertaken. But the individual researcher has played the role not only of the theorist but also of the producer of primary knowledge in many fields. The work of J. B. Mays and D. Downes concerning delinquency and the contributions of Bryan Wilson and David Martin to the sociology of religion are notable examples.[1]

It appears that on the whole research has been proceeding along the lines of a twofold dichotomy: the large-scale nation-wide (often longitudinal) survey and the intensive local study on the one hand; empirical work and theoretical research on the other. We shall argue below[2] that the latter split is detrimental and that there is need for integrating theoretical and empirical research. As far as the former dichotomy is concerned, R. K. Kelsall has pointed out that certain inherent advantages are found in the two broad types of investigation. Thus, the results of the nation-wide survey 'can be linked with other national data from official and unofficial sources, and can be used as the basis of international comparisons'. On the other hand in the local study there is a 'much greater possibility of face-to-face contact between the investigator and the people he is studying, and the much longer period over which the contact can be maintained. This, in its turn, is

[1] It may be noted that many of these contributions have come in the way of Doctors' or Masters' theses.

[2] See pp. 205–7.

likely to mean that the information on *attitudes* is more reliable, and a much more comprehensive picture of the factors influencing the situation can be built up.' As Kelsall says, the two types of study should be complementary.[1] A good example of how this can be achieved is furnished by the first investigation carried out by the Sociological Research Unit at the London School of Economics under the direction of D. V. Glass. The object of the investigation was first of all to provide the general background and framework for the analysis of social differentiation and social mobility in Britain, and secondly to promote more specific enquiries as into the process of recruitment to middle-class occupations. The first aim was achieved mainly through a large-scale nation-wide field study; the more specific studies employed quite different techniques. But these studies had the same purpose and outlook as the basic enquiry, the great merit of which was to provide a general framework, and thus to ensure continuity and integration in the study of social differentiation.[2] The need for a general framework has also been stressed by J. D. Halloran in connection with mass-communication research. He emphasizes in particular the need for theoretically based frameworks and argues that it is a *sine qua non* to link theory with empirical knowledge, a point we shall pursue in our concluding chapter.[3]

Finally we shall look at the way in which sociological research work links up with other social science research.[4]

[1] R. K. Kelsall, *Sociological Research in Britain*, Univ. of Sheffield, inaugural lecture, 30 Nov. 1960, pp. 8, 9.

[2] See D. V. Glass (ed.), *Social Mobility in Britain*, *op. cit.*, ch. 1; D. Lockwood, *The Blackcoated Worker*, *op. cit.*, preface; R. K. Kelsall, *Sociological Research in Britain*, *op. cit.*, p. 11. See also London School of Economics, *Calendar 1962–3*, pp. 524–5.

[3] J. D. Halloran, *Attitude Formation and Change*, *op. cit.*, p. 113.

[4] In this connection the writer is particularly indebted to comments received from Dr Michael Young.

A major impression that readers must have gained from Chapters 3 to 5 is that sociological research has been continually meeting and overlapping with research in other disciplines. One result of this has been the creation of hybrid disciplines such as political sociology, social psychology or criminology. It appears that sociology has invaded and helped to transform other disciplines. As far as research techniques are concerned, it is true that many of these are common property to sociology and the other social sciences; but it is also obvious that sociology has borrowed a number of techniques developed initially by other disciplines, such as participant observation from anthropology or the collection of secondary data from history. It will be argued in the concluding chapter that whatever the origin of these techniques sociology must reshape them and adapt them to its own special needs. In this sense we are in agreement with J. A. Banks who maintains that the main trend in the last two decades has been for sociology to develop into a specialism, and that it is no longer realistic or tenable to regard it as a synthesis of all other disciplines dealing with various aspects of social life.[1] According to this view sociology does not rest simply on the data supplied by other disciplines. Its raw material is often basically the same as that of other disciplines—as, for instance, the phenomenon of division of labour—but whilst the economist would consider this from the point of view of productivity and the psychologist from that of effects on individual personality, the special perspective of the sociologist would be to analyse relations between groups and thus to concentrate purely on the societal aspects of human behaviour.[2]

But this trend to specialization in the social sciences, which is analogous to developments in the natural sciences, does not prevent interdisciplinarity and cross-fertilization. On the con-

[1] J. A. Banks, 'The British Sociological Association—the First Fifteen Years', *Sociology*, vol. 1, no. 1, Jan. 1967.

[2] See Bottomore, *Sociology*, *op. cit.*, ch. 4.

trary, whilst the increasing complexity of each discipline has led to greater specialization the great advance in knowledge has at the same time produced closer links and greater interdependence between various disciplines, even cutting across the dichotomy of 'natural' and 'social' science.[1] Although we have selected mainly studies with sociological orientations, much of the research reviewed involved an interdisciplinary approach, even though this may have been only implicit or rather widely defined. It is clear that where certain aspects of delinquency or Borstal and prison life are examined by the sociologist he must acquire and use some background knowledge about legal arrangements; and where the sociology of industry is investigated, the help of the economics of management may have to be sought. Several examples can be given of units which promote the interdisciplinary approach. The Department of Social and Economic Research at the University of Glasgow is composed of economists, sociologists and representatives of other disciplines such as law and geography. Its main interests are the study of urban, industrial and labour problems as well as regional planning and the Scottish economy. Its approach to research is well reflected in the view that 'Much of the work of the Department might be described as "social-economic", without the "and" which so often divides in an unnatural way the social from the economic'.[2] In another Scottish university an attempt has been made to integrate anthropology and sociology. According to Kenneth Little, with the clarification of concepts, the mutual borrowing of techniques and a convergence in interests, the

[1] See a discussion of these developments in O.E.C.D., *The Social Sciences and the Policies of Governments, op. cit.*, p. 23ff. This trend can be seen also in connection with forecasting in the social sciences: see Michael Young (ed.), *Forecasting and the Social Sciences*, Heinemann for Social Science Research Council, 1968, pp. ix, 19.

[2] See note prepared for the University *Gazette*, no. 47, March 1965, Department of Social and Economic Research, University of Glasgow.

two disciplines are becoming integrated, a trend which is promoted in the Department of Social Anthropology at the University of Edinburgh.[1] Considering the relations between sociology and psychology Gordon Trasler believes in the necessity for continual cross-fertilization between the work of specialists in these disciplines, and we cannot do better than quote, at some length, his reasons for this view at which he arrived through work in the field of criminology. He says: 'It is manifestly impossible to construct a theory of criminal behaviour which would explain even what is at present known about criminals without taking into account empirical information about the structure of families and class differences in social behaviour. Many of the concepts which psychologists use in their study of the individual are also derived from the work of sociologists. In the clinical sphere, too, the psychologist's assessment of the personality of an offender must be related to empirical information concerning the values and attitudes of the group to which he belongs before a practical recommendation can be achieved. If the obligation of the psychologist in this field to the sociologist appears at present rather one-sided, there are indications that it will not always be so. In the development of penal techniques, for example, which will be mainly the concern of the applied sociologist, there will surely be increasing need for methods of conceptualizing and measuring individual differences in responsiveness to social pressures.'[2] Cross-fertilization between psychology and sociology is not, however, evident in the work of some research units even when interdisciplinarity is generally claimed. This appears to be true in the case of the Tavistock Institute of Human Relations. There has been a tendency in the work of this institute 'to explain social phenomena in

[1] Kenneth Little, 'Research Report No. 2', *Sociological Review*, vol. 8, no. 2, Dec. 1960, p. 255.
[2] Gordon Trasler, *The Explanation of Criminality*, Routledge, 1962, pp. 120–1.

psychological terms';[1] and J. A. Banks criticizes the fact that in some of its work, concerned with one of the institute's main fields of interest, i.e. management organization, important sociological contributions are largely ignored, thus detracting seriously from the value of studies emanating from this institute.[2]

A similar view to Trasler's emerges also from J. D. Halloran's conclusions in mass-communications research. He denies the possibility of a deeper understanding of the impact of mass media by a purely sociologistic or purely psychologistic approach. This is not to be regarded as tantamount to reducing one discipline to another. It is, however, the case that a study of this area, even within one discipline, is bound to involve the use of concepts that cut across traditional disciplinary boundaries. A clear case in point favouring the interdisciplinary approach is, for instance, 'the investigation of the relationship between viewing patterns, pre-dispositions and social structure'. But Halloran makes it clear that: 'It is not a case of integrating theories but of linking processes, and although traditional disciplinary levels and boundaries may be crossed in the investigation of specific problems, the disciplines can still have their own distinctive frameworks and theoretical orientations.'[3]

Fruitful collaboration and true interdisciplinarity is seldom achieved even where a joint project is started by social scientists. It is often the case that after the first phase of examination of the field as a whole, a repartition of tasks according to individual disciplines takes place. Each goes on to execute his own part of the research and at best this becomes

[1] Richard K. Brown, 'Research and Consultancy in Industrial Enterprises: a Review of the Contribution of the Tavistock Institute of Human Relations to the Development of Industrial Sociology', *Sociology*, vol. 1, 1967, p. 37.

[2] J. A. Banks in *Sociologische Gids*, Boom and Meppel, Jan./Feb. 1967, pp. 42–3.

[3] J. D. Halloran, *op. cit.*, p. 119.

simultaneous exploration of several aspects of the same topic. It is obvious that in such cases mere lip-service is being paid to interdisciplinarity; the results of each discipline are merely juxtaposed, there being no possibility of integrating the results.[1]

These rather convincing views add much weight to the argument in favour of a multi-disciplinary approach in which sociology must play its role of focusing attention on the societal aspects of human life. The sociologist works, therefore, as a specialist who is entitled to concentrate on the sociological aspects of a topic and to be led by the dictates of his discipline. But where he is fully aware of the contributions that other social sciences can make to the true understanding of human life in society his own contribution becomes the more valuable. And where he collaborates with other social scientists in joint projects he helps even more importantly in the intensification of research efforts endeavouring to raise the standards of our knowledge of human life.

The above viewpoint is on the whole borne out by certain facts and opinions which emerged from a survey about sociological research. Thus, comparing proposed research with current or completed research it was found that the accent has shifted on to team work, particularly of an interdisciplinary kind.[2] The survey also pointed to the view expressed by many sociologists that a relative absence of continuity and cumulativeness still prevailed. This was put down to a lack of

---

[1] See O.E.C.D., *The Social Sciences and the Policies of Governments, op. cit.*, p. 60.

[2] The figures show in fact that there was some increase in research carried out by individuals between 1961 and 1966. However, there was clearly an upsurge of *proposed* team projects, i.e. 62 per cent as against 45 per cent of projects carried out by teams during 1961–6. This may be a sign of the greater financial encouragement which sociology has come to enjoy and of a more mature outlook in the discipline. See 'Report on a Survey of Sociological Research in Britain', *op. cit.*, pp. 9, 19.

research institutes or units, and many stressed the need for more planning and coordination.

In drawing some final conclusions it is hoped that what has been said suggests clearly that the future of sociological research lies in stressing the need for continuity, for integration between individual contributions and team work, and for due regard to the interdisciplinary approach. We shall now turn to some more general comments about the state and needs of sociological research in Britain.

General conclusions

It is perhaps unjustified to attempt to weigh up the achievements and failures of sociological research when such a judgment has to be based on a relatively brief review. Nevertheless some comments may be useful.

On the side of achievements it may be noted that substantive contributions have been made to our knowledge and understanding of social life, through empirical studies which are particularly enlightening for community planning and reorganization, the provision of social services, problems of deviant behaviour, industrial relations, class alignments and race relations. Similarly, the discipline has gained greatly from advanced theoretical work both in specific areas such as social stratification and in more general fields, for instance with regard to the processes of social change. This is a general assessment not based on a detailed evaluation of individual contributions. But it may be pointed out that pieces of research differed both in the degree of originality and the extent to which due regard was given to methodological or theoretical requirements. Some evaluative criticism concerning this kind of unevenness in sociological research was made in the concluding remarks to Chapters 2–4.

Considering, however, the advances and contributions in general terms, we find that on the whole these have been made on parallel lines rather than in a well-integrated form, and this pinpoints the main failure of sociological research in Britain. There has been too much pigeon-holing. The field is probably not as fragmented as W. J. H. Sprott's impression of the different types of sociologist and the general state of the discipline might suggest.[1] For our purpose it is much more

[1] W. J. H. Sprott, *Sociology at the Seven Dials, op. cit.*; see also his *Science and Social Action, op. cit.*, p. 44ff; and see above, pp. 196–8.

pertinent to view the field in the way R. K. Kelsall does, as dichotomized between empirical enquiries and theoretical work.[1] Far too often the studies have shown that there are those sociologists who concentrate mainly on empirical work as distinct from those whose main interests lie in theory. Sprott has also pointed to the lack of connection between empirical work and theory. 'The empirical research of social scientists [tends to be] varied, unrelated the one to the other, and frequently unconnected with social theory.'[2] This split was reflected in quite a number of studies, some of the empirical work lacking sufficient theoretical guidance, while some theoretical treatises verging often on discussion in the abstract without enough attention being given to empirical evidence. As Kelsall quite rightly points out, 'unless theory is underpinned by at least a minimum of essential basic data, it loses much of its value'.[3] And the obvious rider to this is that unless empirical work is guided by theory its results may be sterile. It cannot be stressed too much that without close cooperation between the two sides the discipline cannot truly advance.

The remarkably slender relationship between the development of elaborate theories and the collection of data has been attacked by Peter Townsend. In considering the changes in the institutions of family and kinship in industrial society he demonstrates, in outline form, the way in which theory building is to be based on empirical evidence.[4] J. D. Halloran,

[1] R. K. Kelsall, *Sociological Research in Britain*, inaugural lecture, Univ. of Sheffield, 30 Nov. 1960, p. 5.

[2] Sprott, *Science and Social Action*, *op. cit.*, p. 44.

[3] Kelsall, *Sociological Research in Britain*, *op. cit.*

[4] P. Townsend, 'Family and Kinship in Industrial Society', *Sociological Review Monograph 8*, *op. cit.*, p. 89ff. For a discussion of the limits of *a priori* theorizing see W. G. Runciman, 'Sociological Evidence and Political Theory', in Peter Laslett and W. G. Runciman, *Philosophy, Politics and Society*, Blackwell, Oxford, 1962, p. 42ff; and Tom Burns, *Sociological Explanation*, Inaugural Lecture no. 28, Univ. of Edinburgh, 8 Feb. 1966, p. 9.

writing about mass-media research, similarly draws attention to the necessity for a closer linkage between theory and empirical knowledge, and stresses the truism that 'We are not merely concerned with the collection of facts, we aim at broad generalizations'. 'These', in his view, 'can be developed best if research is conducted within a theoretical framework', and he further emphasizes that 'Exploration to be successful depends on a good theory as a starting point'.[1]

A very good example of a piece of empirical research which started off with a clarification of existing concepts and theories, had a theoretical conception, and led through fieldwork and empirical study to new theoretical conclusions, is the one carried out by Rex and Moore in the area of race relations. Thus, the authors rejected theoretical orientations found in many race relations studies either because they were non-sociological or because they did not seem adequate for the field situation at hand.[2] Subsequently through their empirical study they were able to lead to the crystallization of a theory of race relations in the industrialized urban setting.[3]

These are a few of the clearer examples of awareness among some sociologists that research must be empirically based but theoretically oriented.

There is another aspect of fragmentation which requires correction. Taking the various areas in which investigations have been conducted, the picture is one of a lack of liaison *within* them.[4] Whilst many useful local enquiries have been carried out, in such fields as community studies or race relations, there has been no link between these, with the consequence that the findings are often too diversified to allow cumulativeness. We would concur, therefore, with D. V. Glass'

---

[1] J. D. Halloran, *Attitude Formation and Change*, *op. cit.*, p. 113.

[2] John Rex and Robert Moore, *Race, Community and Conflict*, *op. cit.*, p. 12ff.

[3] *ibid.*, see introduction and ch. 12.

[4] See the discussion generally on integration, above pp. 184, 188ff.

advice that there is a need 'to establish an order of priority in developing systematic research into problems which, as occurs so often in sociology, have hitherto been treated largely on an *ad hoc* basis. In such circumstances, however valuable individual studies may be, the separate studies are either not additive, or at best the process of addition is both difficult and precarious.'[1] What seems to be needed first, as Glass points out, is an 'overall view', even if this would tend to be formal and quantitative. This would provide, however, a sound basis for the qualitative investigations dealing with 'the subtleties of social relationships'. The latter would fit into the general pattern and supplement each other in a way in which haphazardly conceived individual investigations cannot. Thus a more meaningful whole could be produced in any one area in which sociological research is carried out.

It ought to be mentioned here that useful work has been undertaken recently in an attempt to achieve standardization regarding basic descriptive data. A Working Party on the Comparability of Data, led by Margaret Stacey under the auspices of the British Sociological Association, presented five papers concerned with the standardization of such 'key variables' as age, sex, marital status, birthplace, education, family and household, income, and occupation.[2] The aim was to achieve comparability by suggesting to researchers the use of standardized descriptive schemata. It was not envisaged, however, that the adoption of this kind of framework should preclude or constrain the use of individually devised schemes for presenting data.[3] But a concomitant presentation of data within agreed common frameworks would, it was thought,

[1] D. V. Glass (ed.), *Social Mobility in Britain, op. cit.*, p. 10.

[2] The papers were presented at the Conference of the University Teachers of Sociology section of the BSA, at Bedford College 3 Jan. 1968.

[3] See introduction by Margaret Stacey to Papers of the Working Party on the Comparability of Data, Set. 1, Nov. 1967.

enhance the value of studies and provide the 'overall view' which, as mentioned above, is often lacking.

Finally, the review seems to justify a strong plea for more attention to be given to methodology and the improvement of techniques. The contention here is that, although most of the studies paid some attention to the methods and techniques of research, this part of the strategy appeared often to have been relegated to a position of secondary importance. In a sense this is not surprising. For in the normal course of research, where results related to a certain topic or problem other than methodological or 'technical' are expected, the researcher will not be able to devote sufficient time to methodological problems or the improvement of the techniques at his disposal.[1] A certain amount of research must, therefore, be explicitly method- and technique-oriented. In this respect sociological research in Britain is singularly lacking. Apart from a general guide, such as found in John Madge's *The Tools of Social Science*,[2] or an occasional discussion of some one aspect, such as Bryan Wilson's contribution on 'content analysis',[3] very little has been accomplished. In certain areas, as in social statistics, experimental research does occupy an important position, and in America such endeavours have been established long ago and cover wider areas.[4] But there is still much scope, specifically for sociology, in this respect. And it is not too ambitious to envisage this kind of research in Britain in order to give a clear guide, through systematic

[1] Again, not all researchers can be expected to take a deeper interest in the field of methods and techniques.

[2] John Madge's book was published in 1953. Moser's rather more specialized *Survey Methods in Social Investigation* appeared in 1958. An example of a recent American book in this field is Bernard S. Phillips, *Social Research: Strategy and Tactics*, Macmillan, New York, 1966.

[3] Bryan R. Wilson, 'Analytical Studies of Social Institutions', in Welford *et al.*, *Society*, *op. cit.*, p. 99ff.

[4] See appendix, below.

comparison and checking, as to the likely efficacy of different approaches and techniques in sociological investigations.[1] There can be little doubt that the value of much future research could be enhanced in this way.

As a final summing up it is appropriate to stress that the purpose of this review throughout has been neither to provide an exhaustive account of the work sociologists have carried out in Britain, nor to explain in any detail the various research skills they have applied. Rather it was the object to show the main *trends* in sociological research. Another important aim was to direct attention to the more glaring weaknesses of post-war endeavours. Such a critical, and some may claim non-constructive, approach is defensible only if the outcome furnishes some positive suggestions. In the foregoing remarks the immediate needs of the discipline, from which certain general proposals emerge, have in fact been spelled out. In broad outline these are: the acquisition of sounder methods and techniques, the provision of adequate basic frameworks, and the insistence on a close mutual support between empirical and theoretical work.

[1] See some points in this connection in appendix, below

Appendix 1: A note on experimental research in sociological techniques

There are a number of good examples of experimental research carried out in Britain mainly in connection with survey work. Thus, C. A. Moser and A. Stuart dealt experimentally with quota sampling[1] and Kathleen Gales and M. G. Kendall concentrated their inquiries on non-sampling errors 'such as arise, for example, from the fallibility of interviewers, imperfections in questionnaire design, or interaction between interviewer and respondent'. To test such factors comparatively they applied two different types of questionnaire and briefing in their experiment.[2] In America much technique-oriented research has been going on for a long time: for instance, the work of Stuart A. Rice, who was concerned with obtaining objective indicators of subjective variables, and Robert F. Bales, Leon Festinger and others, who looked at the way in which interpersonal relations can be formally analysed.[3] There is need in sociology for experimental research which could draw its leads from the kind of work mentioned here. This is to be undertaken in order to provide the necessary guides to the researcher dealing with non-methodological and non-technical problems. A programme can be envisaged in which a number of tools, such as interviewing, content-analysis and observation, would be compared systematically so as to check their efficacy for different types of sociological study. Many difficulties would no doubt arise. The problem of evaluating the techniques comparatively tested is a very serious one, although

[1] C. A. Moser and A. Stuart, 'An Experimental Study of Quota Sampling', *Journal of the Royal Statistical Society*, Series A (General), 116, 1953, pp. 349–405.

[2] K. Gales and M. G. Kendall, 'An Enquiry Concerning Interviewer Variability', *ibid.*, Series A (General), Part II, 1957, p. 120 ff.

[3] See the contributions of Stuart A. Rice, Robert F. Bales, Leon Festinger and others in Paul F. Lazarsfeld and Morris Rosenberg (eds.), *The Language of Social Research*, Free Press, New York, 1955, pp. 35ff and 345ff.

where objective criteria exist it would be possible to check more accurately the predictive power of each technique. The simplest objective criteria are voting behaviour, against which the predictions of a pre-election survey can be checked, or the act of formally joining an organization, against which findings about people's attitudes to and interests in such an organization can be checked. There is, however, a chance that the objective criteria may be contaminated, which would present a complex problem. Thus interviewing, participant observation and getting secondary material may all arouse interest in a group or organization (political, religious or professional) among its members or potential members. The different techniques may arouse, however, such interest in different directions and degrees and so affect, in a variety of ways, the results of an enquiry about group identification. The very fact that such difficulties exist should have induced greater interest among sociologists in Britain in the field of technique-oriented experimentation. And it is also true that even where objective criteria are difficult to pin down, or where they might be of doubtful value, the mere replication of experiments, or at the very least the checking of techniques used in actual investigations would be valuable. It is for this reason that the Registrar General has asked the Government Social Survey to carry out a Post Enumeration Survey as a follow up to the Population Census of 1966. 'Its purpose is to provide a check on the coverage and quality of work done by Census enumerators.'[1] It is difficult to see why sociological investigations should not be subjected to such experimental checking. The accumulation of knowledge and refinement of skills achieved by this kind of experimentation would eventually help the sociological researcher no end to arrive at the correct decisions in his choice between alternative approaches and techniques. Generally accepted notions about skills not experimentally tested may be totally erroneous. The sociologist must be provided with more definite and more reliable guidelines.

[1] See *Social Science Research Council Newsletter*, November 1967, p. 7.

Appendix 2: Research material and finance

A few details about a smaller and somewhat less representative group of studies may be of some interest. 79 studies composed of 27 theses and 52 books[1] which were used for the first draft of this book were checked regarding the kind of research material they used and the financial support they received.

Considering the material used it was found that in thesis work eight relied mainly on field research, eight on secondary material without any original field work, and the remaining 11 used a combination of secondary and field material. Of the published books 17 relied mainly on field work, 25 on secondary material and 10 on a combination of the two. In total, therefore, 33 of the 79 studies were based on already existing material; 25 adduced fresh material; and 21 used a combination of existing and new material. It was natural to find that for all the theses one individual in each case was responsible for the work done, since this is a university regulation. There were three students, however, who were helped by others (apart from their supervisors) in their research. With the published volumes, on the other hand, 13 studies were carried out with the aid of research teams, nine studies by two or more individuals, and there were 30 publications for which single individuals were responsible.

On the financial front, in the case of 35 of the 79 studies (11 theses and 24 publications) it was clearly noted that fellowships and scholarships or special grants were received.[2] Although this shows that less than half of the studies considered had some form of sub-

---

[1] Only London University theses were taken and the books did not cover the topics of religion and education, and only partially covered criminology and industrial sociology. All were drawn only from the period 1959–64.

[2] It is possible that for some studies, particularly theses, the receipt of grants or scholarships was not mentioned. For a full list of bodies which have made research grants, see below.

vention, according to the Heyworth Committee the sociology group at universities has not fared badly as regards the receipt of outside grants. Thus, with 259 teaching staff and 67 university- or college-financed research staff it received £300,000 in external research funds and had 156 research students and 88 students on advanced courses (both figures relate to British nationals only). In comparison, economics had 584 teaching and 99 research staff, received £167,000 and had 193 research students and 73 on advanced courses. But the Committee says that 'Although economics received from external sources a smaller amount than the sociology group, it is likely that the total research carried out in the subject was about the same because of the much larger number of "teaching" and "research" staff.'[1] Nevertheless the above shows that sociological research has made important strides. At the same time it must be remembered that the Committee mentions nine research institutes which carry out at least a certain amount of sociological research (some almost entirely such research) and which receive financial support from various foundations, the government, industry and private subscriptions.[2] There is no doubt that the need for sociological research is now widely recognized.

List of grant-giving bodies[3] (*state scholarships excluded*) *based on information in 79 studies:*

Arthur McDougall Trust
Australian National University Travelling Research Fellowship
Australian Services Canteen Trust Fund
Bethlem Royal Hospital
Board of Deputies of British Jews
Bristol University
British Sociological Association
Carnegie (U.K.) Trust and Carnegie Trust for the Universities of Scotland
Centre for Urban Studies

[1] Heyworth Committee, *op. cit.*, p. 23.
[2] *Ibid.*, pp. 86, 87.
[3] For more information see *Register of Research in the Human Sciences, 1960–61*, DSIR, HMSO, 1962.

Charles Henry Foyle Trust
City Parochial Foundation
Dartington Hall (Trustees of)
Elmgrant Trust
Ford Foundation
Gloucester Community Council
(Sir) Halley Stewart Trust
Hebrew University–Institute of Contemporary Jewry
Home Office Research Unit
Isaac Wolfson Foundation
Joseph Rowntree Memorial Trust
King George V Jubilee Trust
Leverhulme Trust
Liverpool University, Department of Social Science
London School of Economics Research Bursary and Social Research
    Division
Manchester University
Maudsley Hospital
National Council of Social Service
New Bridge Society
Noel Buxton Trust
Nuffield Foundation
Tavistock Institute of Human Relations
UNESCO
University of Edinburgh, Committee of the Social Science Research
    Centre
University of London, Central Research Fund

Index of subjects

Index of names